And Another

Thing...

...about Living, Loving, and Learning

Carol Goodman Heizer

Alpha Publishing
a division of Alpha Consulting
Louisville, KY

Alpha Publishing
A division of Alpha Consulting

First Printing, October, 1998
Copyright © 1998 by Carol Goodman Heizer

ISBN 0-9656402-4-8
Printed in U.S.A.
Louisville, KY

Library of Congress Catalog Card Number:
97-93487

For information about books, tapes, and seminars, contact:
Alpha Publishing
A Division of Alpha Consulting
P.O. Box 18433
Louisville, KY 40261-0433
Phone (502) 239-0761
FAX (502) 239-0764

Email: cgheizer@welcometoalpha.com
URL: www.welcometoalpha.com

Cover Photo by Broderbund, Novato, CA 97948-6125
Cover designed by Rick Hogue
Inside Photos by Carol Goodman Heizer

Acknowledgements

My special thanks to the following people:

To Elaine Thomas, my editor, for her editing skills and eyes of a hawk;

To Cathy Zion, Terry Meiners, Sue Riley, and Patti McNames for their time and energy in previewing and offering constructive criticism;

To Rick and Holly Hogue, for their format and layout suggestions;

To my family for picking up the slack when I spent more than my share of time away from household responsibilities;

To Spencer, our beloved Beagle, who kept me company during the wee hours of the mornings as I stayed at my computer ... when he and I were the only 2 conscious souls in the house.

My mother, Chleo Anna Deshler Goodman (1913-1976)

She was the woman who not only gave *birth* to me on April 22, 1945 . . . but she also gave *life* to me through her entire existence. She was the one who nursed me through colds and fevers, and she stood by my hospital bed day and night after surgery.

She was the one who was never too busy to answer my questions or "just sit and talk." She was the one who gave to me at the expense of herself.

She was the one who rushed me to the hospital to have my stomach pumped when I climbed up three shelves into a wall cabinet and swallowed heart medicine. She was the one who saw me through the terrible after-effects of eating too many green apples from a neighbor's tree.

She was the one who bandaged my bleeding knees and elbows when I made untimely contact with the sidewalk. She plucked 66 splinters out of my feet when I slid down a telephone pole barefooted.

Mother was the one who left a letter in my dorm room after leaving me on a college campus 500 miles from home reminding me that she was not trying to push me out of the nest, but merely trying to help me learn to use my wings. She told me to set my course on the task that was set before me.

She was the one who wrote another letter four years later, upon college graduation, reminding me that it had not been an easy four years. She went on to caution me that nothing worthwhile in life is easy, for if it were, everyone would win . . . and there would be no special merit in even attempting to run the race.

She was the one who lovingly wrote another letter and left it on my breakfast tray the day I was married. Continuing in her wisdom, she reminded me that on that day, I was to carefully tuck away my carefree childhood dreams and step forth to face the reality of being a wife, home-maker, and eventually a mother. But, she cautioned, I could not let all those thoughts frighten me, for it would be a daily process of learning, trying, making mistakes, and learning from those mistakes.

Mother was the one who, many times over the years, reminded me that LOVE knows only two mathematical processes . . . addition and multiplication. She said it knows nothing of subtraction and division.

Oh, Mother, I wish you were here!

Contents

Foreword

Everyone sees life and reality through the filter of their family and their own experiences. Each of us is an extraordinary combination of heredity and experience. It is this individual perspective of how we interpret events that sets us apart from one another. This outlook creates the uniqueness of spirit that we contribute to the world and through this distinctive interplay of nature and nurture that we define meaning.

All of us come from varying ethnic, religious, racial, economic, and geographic backgrounds, and we interpret life through either male or female perspectives. Yet in many ways we are surprisingly alike. In the course of our lives, most of us have traveled through the chapters outlined in *And Another Thing ... about Living, Loving, and Learning.* We can relate to our homes and the effect that our parents, siblings, friends and teachers had on us. We can relate to the education we received ... both good and bad. We can identify the lessons we learned while in and out of school ... whether those lessons were intentional or not. We passed through, and survived, adolescence. We have established relationships with others. Many of us have children and can relate to both the challenges and rewards that go with the responsibility. We have experienced moments when the death of a loved one or despair over a failed relationship has overwhelmed us.

And Another Thing ... about Living, Loving, and Learning is intensely personal. It deals with individual experience. It is Carol Heizer's effort to make sense out of the experiences that have shaped her life. We are given the opportunity to experience life through her eyes. There is no effort to change these experiences for public consumption. In the chapters of this book, Carol takes us into her confidence. We experience with her the pain of visiting the grave site of loved ones, the joys of reminiscing with old friends, and the heartbreak of seeing the remnants of a past life swirling in devastating flood waters. We learn the conclusions she has come to and the lessons she has learned as a result of her observations.

In sharing her thoughts with us, she (in turn) gives us the opportunity to examine our own lives. It challenges each of us to be as honest and as open with ourselves as Carol has been with herself. How has each of us interpreted the chapters of our lives? Are those interpretations still valid? And if so, what have we learned from them? How do they affect our lives and the way we see the world?

And Another Thing ... about Living, Loving, and Learning is not only about witnessing, observing, and preserving relationships with others. It is about establishing and preserving a relationship with ourselves. Carol Heizer forces us to reflect on our own lives, as she has reflected on hers. Her stories and observations, although intensely personal, share a common thread that weaves through all of our lives as well. As we have all experienced a sunset, each of us has experienced it differently. We will, therefore, each read these essays and apply them to our own reality. *And Another Thing ... about Living, Loving, and Learning* is not the same for everyone, nor was it meant to be. It is a springboard to stimulate your own reflections.

Read. Reflect. And enjoy.

Bradley Howard, Ed.D.

Partner, Howard and Korn

Thompson Mansion, Second Street, East Liverpool, Ohio

... about

HOME
and FAMILY

Wanted: Parents
Qualifications: Courage and Commitment

We most likely stepped into parenthood believing that those cuddly little bundles of joy would arrive with all the necessary characteristics that would qualify them to be the most perfect children in the world. And just think . . . *we* were the fortunate ones chosen to nurture those ideal little offspring.

Those children of ours were going to be pure beyond description. The best behaved children in the entire family. Ideal beyond reason. A model child for the rest of the neighborhood. Immaculately dressed and spit-shined for all occasions. Impeccable manners. Flawless social graces. A rightful resident of the Elysian fields. A true flower in the desert!

But somewhere between the daydreams of angelic beings and the nightmares of 2:00 a.m. feedings, runny noses, and dirty diapers, we came back to reality and just *perhaps* gave thought to what we had truly gotten ourselves into.

We are not talking about not **loving.**

We are not talking about not **caring.**

We are not talking about **regretting our child's birth.**

We *are* talking about the awesome, sometimes terrifying, responsibility that lay before us.

This tiny creature of approximately seven-and-a-half pounds suddenly entered our world, and our entire existence went completely caddy-wampus! Complete pandemonium concerning how cool to make the baby's room. How hot to make the bottles. The pros and cons of using Brand X baby soap as opposed to using Brand Y. How to keep the family pet from licking the new arrival in the face.

Confusion reigned supreme.

And as we sat in the midst of this turbulent whirlwind of thought, we wondered if life would ever be the same again. But then we got a grip on our emotions, put our intellect in gear, and told ourselves that, yes, life would resume to a somewhat normal state after eighteen or twenty years . . . *if* all went well . . . and *if* Junior didn't decide to live at home until age 35!

We tried to remember Barbara Walters' words that "Being a parent is tough. If you just wanted a wonderful little creature to love, get a puppy."

In our desperate moments of middle-of-the-night fatigue and middle-of-the-day questions and chores, we began to think that maybe that puppy idea wasn't such a bad idea after all.

But then we realized that our bundle of joy had not arrived with a return address! We were in this project for the duration! Whatever may come!

There were the expected hurdles. The *un*expected bumps in the road. The unforeseen obstacles that come with raising children. But as this and other little bundles of joy passed through childhood, scratched and clawed their way through adolescence, and managed to survive the teen years . . . was it really that many years ago . . . we loved them more each day.

We then understood what our parents had said, "You will never know how much you can love a child until you have your own." Little beings who had arrived during such fanfare . . . who were forever falling and accumulating scratches and bruises . . . who relentlessly asked for pets . . . who continuously asked "Why?" . . . who never slept when *we* needed sleep . . . who never permitted the family to walk out the door for Sunday church without having to make a pit stop at the potty . . . these little beings became the center of our worlds. Their tears could break our heart. And their smiles could turn raindrops into rainbows.

And all we needed was courage and commitment.

Parenting is NOT a Piece of Cake

At first thought, one would think that being a parent is the most natural task in the world . . . a simple matter of showing love toward, and teaching responsibility to, your very own offspring. However, few jobs in this world are as easy as they appear, and parenting is one of them. We as parents help the development of our children by understanding their basic physical and psychological needs, properly motivating their behavior, and serving as appropriate role models.

The first element that we as biological parents provide, of course, is life itself as our children inherit our physical and mental characteristics. We must not only provide for our own physical well-being but also do all that we can to protect our children from disease and accidents. Providing food, shelter, and clothing are the most basic aspects of existence; children who are denied these fundamentals will not develop at a normal rate or in a normal fashion.

Aside from biological parenting, we also must provide social parenting . . . the actual raising of the child. This includes the meeting of basic psychological and social needs such as love, respect, affection, and consideration for other individuals. Behavioral scientists have observed babies and children who have been given all the necessary physical care that was required for infants their age. Yet they were deprived of the individual attention normally given to young children. These children were found to be deficient in forming personal relationships later in life.

In one particular situation, the babies in both groups were given equal physical attention. However, in the control group, the infants were touched and cuddled only when it was absolutely necessary. As a result, these babies did noticeably worse in physical growth and development. The withholding of individual emotional attention indeed reduced physical maturation.

Yet in considering the above information, we parents must also realize that, although we play a major part in our children's development, we are *not* solely responsible for their individual strengths or weaknesses. Our children were born with certain "bents" in their make-up, and we can change those bents only to a certain degree. We must never forget that our children *do* have the ultimate choice as to the manner in which they will live their lives. Try as we might at certain times, we cannot live their lives for them.

When we love our children, we must show that love through encouragement and guidance and time spent with them. But that love must also be proven through the appropriately administered discipline. **Never abuse. Never oppression. Never punishment borne out of our own frustrations or guilt.** But love-directed discipline that is aimed toward changing the children's undesirable behavior . . . never aimed at the children themselves.

Many individuals do not like the term "punishment," for they feel that such a word indicates a negative atmosphere in which the children are being *caught* for their mistakes. "Discipline," on the other hand, is a more positively accepted term that connotates a loving and learning environment in which the children are being corrected and taught simultaneously. We must always remember that the behavior is the target . . . not the child.

It may encourage us to remember that children who receive consistent guidance and fairly-administered discipline feel increased love and security. This translation is made when children are very small. One of my own children remarked at only six years old, "Mary Ann's mother and dad must not love her very much. They let her do anything she wants."

Now we realize that all parents think they have the brightest and cutest kids that ever walked the face of the earth, but most small children read the message loud and clear that "lack of discipline means lack of commitment and concern." And what a tragic philosophy for children to live under! Even as our children are attempting to push all our buttons in an attempt to do as they please, they want us to be the firmly standing adult in their lives and have the love and the courage to say, "No." They are wanting us to exhibit TOUGH LOVE.

We as parents must do whatever is necessary to remain calm under the stress of our children's conduct so that we can maintain our sense of objectivity and fairness in meeting out the required discipline.

Frequently, parents discover that serving as an appropriate role model for their children is a difficult task; the parents desire to follow one set of guidelines for their actions, while expecting a completely different set of behavioral guidelines for their children. They believe that, because parents are adults and children are children, two sets of guidelines should be in operation. They adhere to the old adage, "Don't do as I do. Do as I say."

But children will see this philosophy as grossly unfair and will rebel at every opportunity. Such rebellion may be very open and easily detected, or it may be secretly carried out behind the parents' backs. As the double standard continues over a period of time, children's sense of unfairness (and the resulting frustrations) will turn to resentment (which will ultimately lead to anger) toward their parents. We must realize that all we say and do as parents strongly affects our children's behavior and self esteem . . . either positively or negatively. Someone once very briefly and aptly phrased this attitude with the statement, "Train up a child in the way he should go, and go that way yourself."

Finally, we come to the matter of our children's entertainment . . . a subject that usually causes much tension between parents and children. In today's society of both parents working, we are often tempted to allow our children to entertain themselves by whatever means they choose. However, any parent with a true sense of responsibility must realize that children are tremendously affected by their toys and games, along with their reading materials and television shows they watch. Children are born imitators, and they will mimic the attitudes and actions of those with whom they spend a great deal of time . . . be it humans or TV characters.

In attempting to determine our effectiveness as parents, perhaps we should ask ourselves the following questions:

- Am I spending quantity and quality time with my children?

- Am I showing sufficient amounts of love and concern?

- Am I administering love-directed and fair discipline to my children?

- Am I taking an interest in my children's friends and activities?

- Am I demonstrating the courage to stand firmly on my convictions in raising my children?

- Am I living a double standard of behavior and expectations in front of my children?

- Am I showering my children with material possessions in an attempt to compensate for my lack of time with them, or am I showering them with *ME*, which can never be replaced with *things*?

- Am I willing to set my priorities in life so that my children, **who are my investment in the future of the world**, will realize that they are of the utmost importance to me?

Who's Watching the Priorities?

In today's fast paced society, we race at break neck speeds to accomplish two days' work in every twenty-four hour period. And we feel guilty when we take a break from the hurried rush to regroup our thoughts and revitalize ourselves. Sometimes we have trouble distinguishing the **urgent** from the **important**. As we attempt to keep up the pace, we often feel that the hurrier we go, the behinder we get.

But perhaps the saddest of all such situations is when the children are cheated out of important time with mom and dad. As we hear many parents express the thought that they spend *quality* time with their children, we wonder if such individuals also realize the necessity of spending *quantity* time with them. As it is with most situations in life, it is not enough to sacrifice quality for quantity. Or vice versa. We must maintain a good balance of both.

Former First Lady Barbara Bush once said, "The trouble with cleaning the house is that it gets dirty the next day anyway. So skip a week if you have to. [Your] children are the most important thing."

What will our reward be if we work around the clock, store up material treasures, and become involved in worthwhile projects if we lose our own children in the process? What will we accomplish if we make great strides in our professions, yet sacrifice our families in the process? Will it be an empty victory, at best?

There is a Hungarian proverb that says, "A child that is loved has many names." But having that love is not sufficient. It must be expressed . . . in words and in deeds.

We must never forget that a parent influences a child more than all the teachers, preachers, and public officials combined. In what seems to be a flash of time, we go from worrying about the scratches our children put on the furniture to worrying about the scratches they put on the car. These years go by so quickly, are so precious, and cannot be duplicated if we realize too late that we have neglected our most valuable investment in the future . . . our children.

Kahlil Gibran, a Lebanese poet, once reminded us that we, as parents, are the bows from which our children (as living arrows) are sent forth into the world.

That is an awesome thought.

Parenting is an awesome responsibility.

Dr. James Dobson, Christian psychologist and counselor, has put the weight of that tremendous endeavor into proper perspective when he reminds us that parenting is the only job in which, when you get to the point that you are pretty good at it, your job is over . . . your children are ready to leave home.

As parents, do we deeply regret some of our words, attitudes, and actions involving our children? Of course we do. Would we sometimes give all our earthly possessions to turn back the clock and do things differently? Most definitely. Does making mistakes mean we do not love our children? Absolutely not.

What we must realize from our child-rearing experience is that we are not perfect parents because we are not perfect human beings. We have made past mistakes in raising our children, and we will most likely make more mistakes in the future. We may even be falling short in our task right now.

But it isn't too late. It is *never* too late to sit down with our children, explain our circumstances, remind them of our weaknesses, and ask them to bear with us as we continue on in the process of attempting to prepare them for the world that awaits them. Remind them that **LOVE** and **ERRORS** *are not equal.*

One final thought . . . have you ever asked your child's forgiveness for your trespasses? Try it. It's a wonderful experience. Their willingness to forgive will amaze you!

Who's in the Playpen

The story is told of an American couple who decided to send a playpen to their friend in Northern Canada who had just given birth to her fourth child. The friend wrote back in appreciation, "Thank you so much for the pen. It is wonderful . . . I sit in it every afternoon and read. The children can't get near me."

We chuckle at such a story and wonder if such an incident truly occurred, or if it was from the imaginary mind of a bedraggled mother. Either way, it proves a vital point . . . there are those times when parents and children need their private space. Nothing will cause parents' hearts to overflow with love and gratitude for their children than to spend a few hours, a day, or a weekend away from them periodically. Such action does not say, "I don't love my children." It doesn't say, "I wish they weren't here." It simply says that we must have those occasional times to ourselves so that we may put all our responsibilities in proper perspective.

We must remember that our perspectives and those of our children differ greatly. Three-year-old Bobby didn't like the routine of his daily scrubbing, especially when soap was used. He had frequently fussed in typical three-year-old fashion until one day, in total frustration his mother asked, "Bobby, don't you want to be nice and clean?"

"Sure," Bobby replied, "but can't you just dust me?"

We do not need, I'm sure, advice on what to do with those private times we occasionally steal for ourselves. But how about some suggestions for parent-child activities that will delight the child and help to bring back the wonder of childhood for the parent?

- Take a walk where there are flowers and enjoy the similarities and differences of each type. Give them names based upon their appearance.

- Play in a pile of fallen leaves and don't worry about leaf pieces in your hair.
- Stroll along the side of a creek and watch for "water critters."
- Collect stones and talk about their characteristics. Give them names, also.
- Go to a park and swing. See who can swing higher.
- Go down a sliding board and feel the breeze in your face.
- Look at the clouds and tell what each cloud reminds you of.
- Walk through a pet shop and watch your child's glee at observing young animal behavior.
- Make a batch of cookies and don't be concerned if they are slightly misshapen. Don't fuss if your child wants to cut out a blue Christmas tree or a green Easter bunny.
- Act out a play using hand puppets.
- Turn chores into a fun activity.
- Go to the lake and watch the ducks. Decide if they look like anyone you know.
- Play a child's board game and don't be *overly* concerned with the rules. But, at the same time, do not let a child win just to win.
- Play rhyming word games.

Such activities may seem trite and insignificant to us adults, but they create lasting memories for our children.

I recently asked my son Mark (now a young man) what he

liked best about being home with mom during those pre-school years. He surprised me when he remembered, "Sailing leaf boats in the creek."

What *was* "sailing leaf boats in the creek"?

Had we built little boats out of some wonderful material? No.

We merely picked a leaf from the ground, dropped it into the creek, and watched it float down its watery path. Sometimes we tried to keep up with it as it began its journey, but it often left our sight before long.

Was the activity expensive? Hardly.

Did it require creative imagination? Not much.

Did it require preparation time? Not at all.

Was it worth the effort? You bet. Because in the mind of a little pre-school boy, it left lasting impressions of something that was so much fun to do, and he still remembers it as a twenty-year-old young man!

Remember, we must take time to enjoy our children. We must also take time away from them occasionally. And if we remember these two bits of advice, **we** will have to spend less time in the playpen.

Too Old for a Teddy Bear?

Teddy bears are our truest friends. They hug us when we're lonely and comfort us in the dark. They love us when we feel unlovely and listen to us when we truly need a friend. Even when they lose their stuffing, their gentle presence reassures us that some things in life never change.

But why are they called teddy bears?

Why were they not named Frank bears or George bears or Henry bears or Billy bears?

On a cold and blustery day in November of 1902, U.S. President Theodore Roosevelt (more commonly known as *Teddy*) found it necessary to travel south to attempt to settle a border dispute between Mississippi and Louisiana. The President chose to mix some pleasure with his business trip and thus decided to do some hunting in a part of the country that was known for its bear population.

But as luck would have it, no bears were spotted for the first portion of that particular day that would eventually make its eternal mark on American history. During the afternoon, the President received word that there was a bear nearby. What Roosevelt did *not* expect to see was the old bear tied to a nearby tree.

Roosevelt's sportsmanship and sense of fairness took center stage as he refused to have any part in taking a bear under such circumstances. He insisted that his companions untie the bear and let him go.

Meanwhile, back in Washington, the political cartoonist for the *Washington Post* began receiving bits of information concerning the hunting expedition. Needless to say, the cartoonist took advantage of the opportunity to promote this more tender side of the President by continuing to use a bear in future cartoons concerning Roosevelt. After a while, the furry critters became known as *Teddy's Bear.*

Although no written documentation has been located to authenticate the following, it may have some true merit. At the time the story about Roosevelt and the bear was breaking around the world, a German toymaker was busy developing a stuffed bear for children. Through a series of events, the toy maker's bear was displayed at a European trade fair. As the bears began being shipped to the United States, they were first dubbed as "Teddy's Bear, direct from Germany."

Seeing a golden business opportunity, the founders of the Ideal Toy Company began producing bears and, after having gained permission from the President to use his name, began calling their new creation **"Teddy Bear."** And since that time, teddy bears have served a vital role in the lives of children across our nation . . . to children of *all* ages.

Nearly every newborn babe receives at least one bear, sometimes several. The bears become a source of comfort and companionship as children pass through the Terrible 2s, Treacherous 3s, Fearless 4s, Frantic 5s, Stressful 6s, and so on. But lest we think a teddy bear's appeal has age limits, we must recall the many times we have seen them in teenagers' bedrooms, and even in the collections of fully grown adults.

In our modern era, bears come in a multitude of sizes, shapes, and colors.

The medical field realizes the importance of teddy bears in the healing process. Many years ago when our son Mark was nine years old, he was facing surgery on his knee after a dirt bike accident. Needless to say, he was in a lot of pain and very frightened. As my husband and I anxiously awaited Mark's return from surgery, we were delighted to see that the hospital had provided a small bear (tucked into the crook of his arm) to begin the comforting process even as Mark awakened from the anesthesia.

Think back to your own teddy bear. What color was he? How large was he? Did he have button eyes or sew-on eyes? Did his ears stand tall, or did they fall to one side? Was he especially soft and cuddly, or was he stuffed with harder materials?

And of course he had a name. Do you recall what it was? Remember all those secrets you told him . . . things you wouldn't even tell your best friend. He never judged you, made fun of you, or told you all the things you were doing wrong. He was never angry at you, and he *never* made you feel unwanted. He was a special part of your life. And you were a special part of his life.

At some point in history, Teddy Bear was likely demoted to a cardboard box, or perhaps even sent to the attic for storage. Do you know where he is today? If so, why not go and get him, and take a trip down "memory lane" into the past. Visit the days when you and Teddy were an inseparable duo. It doesn't matter how old he is or how ragged he looks.

Simply concentrate upon all the memories he holds inside, just waiting for you to visit again. Was he so loved and cuddled that he is now torn? That's okay. The love he has inside him won't fall out!

Baby Helicopters

My friend Dell Bowen recalls that her middle son, affectionately known as T-BIRD, spent his days searching the skies with binoculars. His anticipation would build with each passing hour, hoping that a plane would cross the sky and come into his field of vision. T-Bird had told his parents ever since the age of three that he wanted to spend his life as a pilot.

The year was 1965, and the family was enjoying a day of picnicking with friends during a wonderful Georgia summer. The children were playing along the lakeshore, enjoying the sun and sand, perhaps building their castles along the beach.

As the adults discussed the various topics that adults discuss at a picnic, little T-Bird came running toward them as fast as his little legs could carry him. His excitement was contagious, and he could hardly contain his joy. His eyes twinkled and danced at the sight of magic sparkles on the water that wonderful afternoon.

T-Bird's joy had been made complete. His dream had come true. He had received the desire of his heart. For on that hot Georgia day, he had found a precious flying machine.

With all the glee and wonder of a three-year-old, T-Bird shouted, "Mommy, Mommy, look at the baby helicopters!" And as all mothers do, Del ran after her son to share in his dream.

She could not imagine.

She had neither seen nor heard aircraft overhead.

But her attention had been on the adults' conversation, and perhaps she had missed their approach.

Yet before her eyes, there they were! In all of their majesty and might flew the high-tech, maneuverable baby helicopters.

To T-Bird, they were, indeed, shining helicopters . . . miracles of flight.

To Del and the rest of the family, they were *dragonflies!*

Only the mind of a child could see beyond the insect to the wonderful world of flying machines. Only the mind of a child could step beyond realism and relish the ideal.

And what about T-Bird? Did he pursue his dreams of flying? Today, at age 35, and more professionally known as Tay, he is . . . of course . . . a commercial pilot.

Ma and Pa

My family was small in numbers on my mother's side, but what I lacked in *quantity*, I made up for in *quality*. I was blessed with wonderful grandparents into my adulthood and two **great-grandparents** until I was seven years old. And great they were . . . loving, caring, hard-working folks from German stock, better known as the Kesselring clan.

I had only one cousin from my mother's family, and we had a true love-hate relationship. Dick was five years older than me, and he delighted in teasing me. I loved being with him, but I hated it when he made me the object of his creative "big cousin-little cousin" games. I suppose his inventiveness was sparked even more by the fact that we were of opposite genders. But one thing Dick and I had completely in common was our love of spending time at our great-grandparents' home in Marietta, Ohio.

Dick always referred to our great-grandparents as Grandma and Grandpa Kesselring, but I somehow began calling them Ma and Pa. That always bothered my mother, for she felt those names sounded terribly disrespectful. But I could not imagine what she meant because I felt such love for them, and I appreciated every moment I could spend in their presence. So Dick continued to call them Grandma and Grandpa. And I continued to call them Ma and Pa.

Many years later, my parents could not believe I had such vivid memories of those wonderful times and, during a college break, we went to Marietta. They had asked me to point out Ma and Pa's house as we drove by, convinced I could never remember. As we drove up and down the streets of the little neighborhood, nothing looked familiar . . . until we turned onto a particular street. Things looked very different, and I was beginning to wonder if I could join the past and the present together. But one house seemed to leap from its property and shout, "Hey! Stop! Remember me?"

And I knew! I knew it was Ma and Pa's house! I'm not sure *how* I knew . . . a lot of structural changes had been made. But I knew. My parents tried to make me think I was mistaken, but it was useless.

I knew, and I *knew* I knew!

The open farm land across the street from the house now held part of a subdivision. That was sad. I wonder if any of the folks living in those homes ever sensed the wonderful times Dick and I had running through the open fields, hiding in the tall growth? I wonder if they ever had an awareness of the many evenings Dick and I had sat with Ma and Pa on the porch as we watched the sun setting on the horizon?

The little country store down the street was also gone, and in its place stood a new home. Somehow that home didn't seem to belong there . . . I wanted the store to be there. That little country place of business where folks gathered to chat and pass the time of day.

In my memory, the little store had the overhanging roof and wooden support posts. And I shall always remember the wooden-slatted sidewalk in front . . . just like a walk down the streets of a television western town. Of course, there were the wonderful treats inside! Especially the tall glass candy counters that held such delectable goodies! It was the high point of our day for Pa to give Dick and me each a nickel and tell us to spend it on whatever we wanted! We would strut down to that little store feeling as though we were millionaires. And no decision on Wall Street was ever made with more thoughtful consideration than those decisions Dick and I made concerning which candy treats to buy. We tried to buy as many candies as we could that sold "2 for a penny" so that we could divide them and have as much variety as possible.

And those little brown sacks that held our treasures! I'm not sure those little brown candy sacks are even available in today's society. They seem to represent an economic era from the past that represents how much a nickel could buy.

Then there was the porch that ran along the side of Ma and Pa's house. Porches played such a vital part in the neighborhood social life in those days that not only did most houses have them in the front and back of the house, but some houses had them that ran along the side for additional gatherings. The adults would talk, and the kids would play on that porch. It became a family museum of treasured memories!

Dick and I were city kids, and we obviously didn't know *anything* about country living. I guess Ma forgot that the day she invited us to come along to the chicken house when she collected what would become the evening meal. When she placed that chicken on the tree stump and lopped off its head with her hatchet, I was not prepared to see the body go running around the yard. I did not realize that what I was witnessing was simply muscle reactions, and that the chicken was feeling no pain. To this day, I can remember screaming, "Ma! Ma! You didn't kill it! It's still alive!"

Poor Ma. She instantly realized her error in allowing me to watch. She snatched me up in her arms, hustled me into the house, and lovingly attempted to explain the physical reality of what I had just seen. But I think Ma regretted that episode until the day she died. And as much as I loved that dear old lady, I **never** went near that chicken coop again. Come to think of it, she never *asked* me to go near it again. And from that day forth, I had a vivid understanding of the phrase, "Running around like a chicken with its head cut off."

Back then, kids didn't get the candy treats they get today. Our treats were fresh fruits and vegetables. Ma and Pa loved mashed potatoes, and the family could count on having them at nearly every evening meal. So when Ma would begin peeling the potatoes, Dick and I would appear out of nowhere. We had been told by our parents not to ask for food, and we obediently complied.

We didn't ask.

We merely sat beside Ma, probably with that drooling "puppy dog" expression that kids still use today when they are wanting something special. She knew how much Dick and I loved raw potatoes, so she gave us the first two potatoes after we magically appeared at her side. And we didn't even have to ask!

Along with fixing potatoes, Ma was an expert at fixing huge pots of green beans, too. I'm sure that's where Dick and I learned to love raw green beans.

We followed our predictable pattern of suddenly appearing.

Ma followed her predictable pattern of giving us raw beans.

And everyone was happy.

I remember the layout of most of Ma and Pa's house, but I especially remember the kitchen . . . and the *l-o-n-g* table that seemed to go on forever. Many family members were present for these wonderful gatherings, and that table was big enough to accommodate all of them. Maybe there was something magical about it that permitted it to grow longer as the need arose.

Sometimes we would have one or more strangers in our midst, as the town vagrants knew that Ma had a tender spot in her heart for the less fortunate. She would never give them money, for she would not contribute to any unsavory habits they might indulge in. But she would always feed them. And she always made them feel part of the family.

Oh, how I wish I could turn back the hands of time. If I could, I would turn them back to those memorable days of family . . .

and love . . . and home-grown/home-cooked food . . . and long porches . . . and strangers at the dinner table . . . and cousins playing the funny little games of childhood. I would even turn back the hands of time to the evenings when Dick and I would get our two glass jars and catch lightning bugs in Ma and Pa's front yard. Pa had punched holes in the lids for us, for we always turned the bugs loose at the end of the evening. And Pa would often sit on the porch and watch us in our bug-catching endeavors.

And finally I understood why my bugs kept disappearing every time I went in the house to go to the bathroom.

Dick kept turning them loose. He didn't put them in his jar. He wouldn't cheat like that. He just kept turning all my lightning bugs loose because he knew it drove me nuts. Once I decided to take my jar into the house with me, but Ma stopped me at the front door with the stern admonition, "I love you. But there will be no bugs in my house."

And the strangest thing about the disappearing bugs incidents . . . every time I asked Pa about it, he never seemed to have seen anything. Do you suppose he and Dick had some sort of agreement between the two of them?

Natural Bridge State Park, Slade, Kentucky

. . . about
TODAY'S
WORKING WOMAN

Thinking to the Beat of a Different Drummer

In ancient societies, women remained at home, received no formal education, had no power (social, economic, or political), and were married and began raising children soon after puberty. Although medieval women were given somewhat more freedom, their lives were dominated first by their fathers and then by their husbands. In more modern times, women continued to work primarily in and around the home until the Industrial Revolution of the 1800s when a shortage in the male workforce brought an increased number of women into the workplace.

As the gender face of the workforce changed and more women began working outside the home, they received more formal education, thereby increasing their employment opportunities. This change came slowly, however. And it came painfully. Nevertheless, as late as the 1950s and '60s, U.S. women considering a profession traditionally were channeled into either hairdressing, secretarial, nursing, or teaching specialties. But today's woman is contributing to, and benefiting from, such career challenges as politics, medicine, law, sports, flight, writing, space, engineering, and publishing.

As we contemplate a woman's changing role over the centuries, we must ask ourselves what it is within some women's internal mechanism that permits them to think beyond the societal confines imposed on them at any given time. What is it within her that causes her to rise above the status quo and accept the challenge of being *more* and *different*. Of being what she *wants* to become, rather than what society *expects* her to become?

Perhaps it is a SENSE OF CURIOSITY, borne out of an intensely inquiring nature that wants to take the already-known and extend it into the realm of the yet-to-be-discovered. As she begins this journey, today's woman is dedicated to finding the 5 W's — who, what, where, when, and why — of the world around her. And the world within her. She asks herself, "*Can* I do this?"

Perhaps it is a SENSE OF CREATIVITY, borne out of an intensely fertile imagination that wants to take the original and bring into being a deeper and higher level of skills and talents and contributions to her world. As she begins this birthing process, today's woman may not be consciously aware of this creative process, but she knows she must take the abilities she has and create something even more inventive and resourceful. She asks herself, "*How* can I do this?"

Perhaps it is a SENSE OF ADVENTURE, borne out of an intensely mundane routine that wants to break free of stagnation and inaction that threatens her very nature as an inventive, spontaneous, and productive creature. As she begins this trek into the unknown, today's woman realizes that dangers and unexpected trials await her, but she also realizes that she can grow and learn from such elements. She asks herself, "How *soon* can I do this?"

Perhaps it is a SENSE OF COURAGE, borne out of an intensely brave inclination that has carried her through difficult trials since the beginning of time . . . an inclination which now must progress forward in her growing awareness and existence. As she departs from her harbor of familiarity and safety, today's woman understands that there are waiting circumstances which will test her spirit, her heart, and her soul. But she knows from the depths of her being that she *must* begin this venture if she is to be true to herself and all that she believes in. She may ask herself, "*Why* am I doing this?", but she answers herself, "Because I, in my resolute desire to accomplish this endeavor, am willing to test my mettle in the test of fire."

Thus, armed with the helmet of curiosity, the belt of creativity, the sword of adventure, and the shield of courage, today's woman embarks upon her voyage . . . braving the elements she knows awaits her . . . in her quest to find her dreams and fulfill her aspirations.

Daycare Nightmare

Each new mother feels that her infant is the most precious baby to ever appear upon earth, and the love she feels toward this tiny stranger who immediately turns her world upside down is overwhelming. But along with this flooding emotion of adoration, new mothers also experience frustrating adjustments, dreams of their child's future, and concerns for their general well-being.

But today's 1.7 million mothers (with children less than one year old) who now constitute today's American workforce must face an additional anxiety. It can appropriately be called the **Daycare Nightmare,** for it involves mothers taking their precious children and leaving them in the daily care of individuals whom they sometimes hardly know.

As numerous horror stories of poorly equipped, insufficiently staffed, and immorally-and-abusively-run operations surface in our news medias, working parents become alarmed over their children's caregivers. And rightfully so, considering that a recent report in *Time* magazine (2/3/97) revealed that 40% of daycare centers gave infants and toddlers less than the minimal standard of care. There are steps that may be taken to lessen the possibility of such shocking and monstrous incidents occurring.

We as parents have the moral and legal obligation to ensure our children's safety . . . physically, emotionally, mentally, and spiritually. And we must fulfill that parental obligation as thoroughly as possible. As we begin our search for a caregiver, we must realize that we may choose from a daycare co-op, family daycare, center care, nanny care, or foreign Au pair care. Obviously, the most reassuring referrals usually come through personal recommendations of family, friends, and coworkers. However, if that is not possible, parents can contact Child Care Aware (1-800-424-2246). This is a national hotline that provides referrals to local resource agencies.

Needless to say, the majority of parents are searching for a children's caregiver who offers more than merely the basic licensing requirements. If this is the goal, there are two quality organizations that can be contacted: the National Association for the Education of Young Children (1-800-424-2460) and the National Association for Family Child Care (1-800-359-3817).

Parents' need for a safe and secure setting for their children's care has resulted in the surgence of the daycare co-op, where members exchange equal baby-sitting time with no monetary expense. Such an arrangement is based upon the members' similar childcare philosophies, consistent care quality, geographical locations, and work schedules. Members pay annual dues, elect officers, and establish a regular meeting schedule to keep lines of communication open and create or enhance friendships among the members. Due to the rise in the co-op's popularity, several publications are available that spell out specific guidelines for creating and maintaining such a program.

Although parents tend to think that a home situation is more emotionally and physically sustaining for their children, while a center is more business-like, such is not always the case. Each situation must be observed and evaluated individually. Preliminary phone calls may begin the choosing process, but only on-site visitations can reveal the true atmosphere. If the caregiver seems intent upon setting a prescribed appointment time (with no allowance for drop-in visits), it *may* indicate a concern of being observed on the spur of the moment. Parents would be wise to reconsider such an environment.

Parents should question potential caregivers concerning their child-rearing thoughts and operating principles. If there is a noted difference between the parents' and the caregivers' philosophies, the children will suffer as they constantly adjust to two opposing views of what is expected of them.

While genetics, nutrition, and the mother's health play a vital role in the brain development of her child, scientists have been discovering that the stimuli a baby receives also plays an equally vital role in their development. Neuroscientists have proven in recent years that the electrical activity of brain cells produced by stimuli actually changes the physical structure of the brain That is an especially distressing fact considering that 1 out of every 10 children in our society today lives at or below 50% of the federal poverty level . . . and lack of personal, social, and educational stimulation and opportunities that come with that poverty level.

The physical surroundings in a quality caregiver environment must not only be clean, wholesome and health-promoting, but it must also be pleasantly and moderately conducive to audio, visual, and kinesthetic stimulation; babies learn and have a greater understanding of the world around them when they are encouraged to explore it with all their senses of seeing, hearing, smelling, tasting, and touching.

In some centers, children stay with the same caregiver for a year, rather than being placed in a new group because of a birthday. Children must have consistency for maximum security, and having daily contact with the same caregiver provides that security. Inquire as to the turnover rate of employees, for a constantly-changing staff may also fuel a sense of insecurity among young children. A child's functioning foundation is largely built upon interpersonal relationships and communication.

Communication not only involves the verbal language, but also such body language as open affection and attention, playfulness, and smiles from the caregivers. When this positive reinforcing communication is given, the children feel safe and comfortable, thereby enhancing their overall ability to absorb and learn in a caring environment.

Recent evidence from Baylor University's College of Medicine reveals that children who do not actively participate in a lot of play or are seldom touched develop brains that are 20-30% smaller than normal size for their age category. And such development or *lack of* development is not limited to human beings. Laboratory animals who are raised in a toy-strewn environment are capable of more highly complex behavior than animals who are deprived of such stimulation.

A list of questions may be addressed by the concerned parents that would include such aspects of child care as:

- Have you checked your local consumer protection office for licensing laws in your city, county, or state?
- Is the caregiver properly licensed?
- What are the current credentials?
- Do the caregivers have references?
- Do the caregivers have special training in child development/education?
- Has your local Better Business Bureau had any complaints about the organization?
- What is the ratio of caregiver to child other than at drop-off and pick-up times?
- Does the center have a high staff turnover?
- Are you introduced to new caregivers?
- Have all caregivers had a criminal records check?
- Are caregivers warm and nurturing toward the children?
- Are caregivers patient with parents who find it difficult to leave their children at first?
- Do the caregivers seem to truly enjoy being with the children they are attending?

- Do the caregivers tell you what your child did that day or what they are in the process of learning?
- Do caregivers see play as a valuable tool in learning?
- Is there sufficient play space both inside and outside the building?
- Is the outside play area fenced?
- Are there separate locations for differing activities, such as eating, sleeping, playing, and diaper changing?
- Is there a storage area for children's personal items?
- Are there comfortable areas for one or two children to be alone together?
- Are furniture and equipment the proper size for children?
- Do the children generally display a sense of contentment and satisfaction?
- Do caregivers engage in two-way conversation with the children?
- Are children encouraged to make decisions and learn independence?
- Are children encouraged to creatively express themselves through art or music?
- Are the children's pictures or projects displayed and changed frequently?
- Are care and behavior quidelines clearly expressed?
- Are all guidelines followed consistently?
- What is the specific discipline procedure?
- Does the child talk in a positive manner about the program and workers?

- What is the policy concerning a sick child being brought to the facility?

- What is the emergency medical procedure?

- When parents find it necessary to call the caregiver, will they be able to speak to an individual, or will they customarily be placed on an answering machine?

- What special considerations are given to mothers who want to breast-feed their children?

- What are the safety precuations in case of fire or other emergencies?

- What toilet-training method is used and at what age?

- What are the nutritional provisions?

- Are special dietary needs addressed?

- Are facilities clean?

- Is good hygiene practiced?

- What are the fees for partial-day or overtime care?

Perhaps one of the greatest concerns for working mothers is that their children will have a lesser bonding capability with them if they are placed under another individual's care during working hours. This is a personal philosophy that varies from mother to mother, but what *all* mothers can do to maximize their relationship with their children is to spend *quality* and **quantity** time with them in order to foster and deepen that mother-child bond that should carry each of them through a lifetime.

Parents have customarily read to their children for many different reasons. One of the primary reasons has been the introduction of vocabulary to children as they hear sounds repeated. Researchers have recently not only realized the benefit from parents reading to their children, but they have also established a definite link between children who are read to and those children's attitudes and accomplishments later in life. The children who have had the benefit of being read to have:

- ☞ a stronger foundation for later reading skills,
- ☞ feelings of closeness and attachment to those around them.

A child who is read to is receiving a good counter-balance in today's world of technology where individuals are becoming more detached from one another. In today's world, we communicate with fellow humans through technological equipment as frequently as we do through personal contact. Reading to children is a simple and inexpensive, yet pleasurable, way of improving our children's physical and developmental health. It is irrelevant whether the reading takes place in a valued family rocker, on the child's bed, on the porch swing, or under a favorite shade tree. Reading can be enjoyed in the family living room or in the city park. The most important advantage of reading to children is the development of interpersonal relationship skills children form as a result of the activity.

We must not only care for our children's physical needs, but we must also share those precious times that cultivate **closeness** and **love** and **trust** and **curiosity** and **truth** and **discipline** and **courage** and **faith** within our children. Such growth is not the responsibility of the childcare provider. Nor is it the responsibility of teachers or preachers or society in general. It is *our* responsibility as parents. And when we accept that responsibility, we will come one step closer to enjoying a rich and rewarding relationship with our children.

Babies are not born as blank chalkboards as doctors once believed, but rather they have measurable brain activity as early as 10 to 12 weeks after conception. Since such activity is present *before* birth, is it not our responsibility to continue to stimulate those 100 **billion** brain neurons that are present at birth?

Should we not be concerned that these are our CHILDREN we are talking about?

And they are our future!

The Ultimate Juggling Act:
Balancing One's Family, Career, and Self

Today's working woman is required to have the balancing skills of a high-wire walker that Barnum and Bailey would be proud to employ. She must divide herself between her family and her career, while at the same time reserving sufficient time, energy, and satisfaction for herself. If she is not sufficiently trained and prepared for her tight-rope walk, disaster lurks in the wings. And if her attention to detail is not properly focused, the results can be devastating.

As women have ascended the ladders of success in the working world, they have experienced increased expectations, expanded responsibilities, and heightened stress. As these situations have stretched many women nearly to their limits of endurance, they are simultaneously faced with the never-ending responsibilities of maintaining a home and family. And under the staggering weight of these two loads, today's working woman must realize the ever-present need to safeguard and preserve her own identity.

Although current times have brought about improved working conditions for women in many respects, we are quite aware of the continued existing discrimination in numerous situations. In an attempt to counter-balance that perspective, today's working woman is finding herself in the position of frequently having to work longer and harder than her male counter-parts to prove her skills and talents. And as her physical, mental, and emotional clock ticks away at lightning speed, she finds herself forgetting to adequately take care of herself so she can provide for her own well-being, in addition to providing for the well-being of those around her.

Although the vast majority of today's working women are totally committed to their job performance, we must remember that there are limits as to what we *can* and *will* do in order to achieve desired goals. We must maintain the freedom to express ourselves when the burden of expected performance becomes too heavy to carry. It is not a sign of weakness. It is not a sign of laziness. It is a sign of human necessity.

Also, many of today's working women are single parents, existing under the tremendous weight of raising children without the help of a partner. Or women may be sharing the domestic responsibilities of child-rearing and home-tending with their husbands; but it is the women who normally carry the bulk of domestic onus. If there are no children involved, the women may feel a somewhat lighter load, although many are caring for elderly parents.

And in the midst of this multi-dimensional struggle, today's working woman is finding less and less time for herself. As her days seem to become shorter and more hectic, she sets aside her own needs and desires in order to focus upon the needs and desires of those around her. In the midst of trying to be all things to all people, she is losing herself; her own identity is becoming buried.

But there are alternatives to this potential downward spiral. First, we must recognize that we, too, are human beings who *must* have our own needs met if we are to continue supporting those around us. Such relaxation and rejuvenation may take the form of physical exercise or jogging to raise the basal heart rate. During these times of physical activity, the endorphins which are released into the body by the brain create a natural heightened sense of well-being and satisfaction . . . a drugless "high" which results in nothing but positive benefits. Necessary revitalization may also come from participation in hobbies or various favored pastimes. Whatever the activity, it must be one that brings about a personal sense of satisfaction and encouragement.

We must also not overlook the mandatory ingredients of proper diet and rest. Most fast-foods and quickly-prepared meals are high in sodium, starches, and fat grams. These not only add needless weight, but they tend to make the human body feel extremely sluggish and unproductive. The name of the healthy game is fresh fruits, vegetables, and grains!

When responsibilities tend to overwhelm us, the first thing we sacrifice is usually sleep. We cannot do this, for we must remember that it is sleep which strengthens, heals, and revitalizes the human body. The game of sleep-catch-up when we finally become exhausted is *not* the remedy. Our nightly sleep habits must be consistently executed if they are to maximize our daily performance.

It is all right to say:

I AM WOMAN.

I AM INVINCIBLE.

I AM TIRED!

(And then proceed accordingly!)

Teton Mountain Range, Wyoming

. . . about

MOTHER NATURE

Listen to the Rocks

The afternoon was spent sitting on a large boulder that jutted out from the mighty rushing water of a mountain stream. The water was as frozen liquid, and its coldness bit into my feet like a bear's teeth. The water's thundering roar seemed to drown out all other sounds as it stampeded its way down its rocky trail. Nothing seemed to exist except the brilliant blue sky, the fluffy white clouds, the blowing trees, the foaming water, the rocks, and myself. And I began listening to the rocks.

I listened as they told their tales of old . . . how they were part of the life-giving source of drinking water for both man and beast. How some of them had been dislodged from their original homes by the rushing water and trembling earth. How their physical features had changed over the years by the force of the water constantly flowing over and around them.

Some of the rocks spoke of the comfort and warmth that were provided by the thick blanket of lush moss covering their exterior.

Some of the rocks shared their sense of pride at possessing such smooth, symmetrical beauty . . . while others boasted of their sharp ruggedness. Some of them remembered their pleasure at seeing the beautiful trout passing through their area, while others spoke of their sense of satisfaction at providing protection for the little stones lying at their base.

One rock in particular shared its sense of enjoyment for providing a safe resting place for the tangled piece of driftwood that had somehow safely lodged against it. This rock felt a particular sense of responsibility for keeping its visitor secure . . . providing a wonderful contrast to the surrounding rocks and water.

One family of rocks explained their gift of hospitality at providing a welcome retreat for the entwining mass of tree roots that existed in their midst.

Finally the rock upon which I sat spoke. It expressed its delight that one would venture so far out into the rushing water to rest a while and soak in the wondrous nature . . . most folks, it said, stayed closer to the shore and the safety of soil.

As I continued to sit and permitted my mind to drift into mental freedom, it was as though all the rocks began giving forth their secrets . . . that finally they had found one who could, and **would**, take the time to allow a relationship to develop. As the thunderous water continued pouring on all sides, I could sense the thoughts and dreams the rocks had absorbed over the centuries.

From the rocks, I heard the fears and uncertainties of the first pioneers as they hacked and chopped their way through the mountain's dense growth . . . and the fatigue those men and women must have felt as they saw yet another rocky, rushing stream they must cross.

I heard the delight of children as they had joyfully jumped from one rock to another, apparently defying the laws of slippery surfaces and gravity.

I heard the dreams of newlyweds as they had romantically slipped away from the crows to find their own temporary paradise . . . ready to embark upon life together, feeling so prepared to face the world together as a team, yet so completely oblivious to the trials that lie ahead.

I heard the relaxation of parents as they briefly paused upon the rocks and escaped from the cares of everyday life and the anxieties of raising a family.

I heard the questions of middle aged folks as they found rocks closer to the shore and snatched a few moments of time from the hectic world in which they functioned. Those folks recalled the times in their younger years when they, too, would have ventured further into the rapids . . . but now they were aware of their declining agility when rock-hopping. I heard the sudden quietness within their homes since the children left the nest . . . the quietness that once was so desired which now seemed so overwhelming. I heard the uncertainty these folks were feeling as they neared retirement and suddenly had questions as to the adequacy of their financial preparations for that inevitable event.

But perhaps, saddest of all, I heard the concerns of older ladies and gentlemen who had already experienced the onset of medical problems. I heard the concern of how they would cope with those problems, both physically and financially. Even greater than the concern, I heard the anticipated loneliness that the remaining spouses would endure after the loss of their beloved partners. But above their concern and anticipated loneliness, I heard the gratitude and appreciation for a love that had been shared over the years . . . a love that had endured the daydreams and nightmares, the pleasures and pains, the ideal and the real of daily life.

As I quietly, almost reverently, left the place that had become so very special . . . so personal . . . to me during that afternoon, I continued to listen to the rocks.

No Sunrise Without a Night

Many of us have had the wondrous privilege of watching the early morning sun as it quietly crawls from its bed to brighten yet another day for each of us. We have stood in awe as we watched the sky transformed from overshadowing darkness into the spectacular splendor of reds, pinks, oranges, and golds as we see those wondrous colors sweep across the eastern horizon. We have thus been a witness to the quiet snuffing out of night.

We reveled in the quiet beauty of an exquisite sunrise, yet we have seldom paused to consider the fact that there would be no splendid dawn without the preceding dismal darkness.

And from this daily beauty, we see again a distinct parallel between Mother Nature and *human nature.*

As we travel back in time over the various periods of our lives, we understand the wisdom of the old adage, "You never appreciate the water 'til the well runs dry." We take our blessings for granted and assume that all will continue to be well with the world. Yet it is during those dark nights of life when trials and turmoil overtake us that we truly grasp the plentitude of all we have been given.

Why is it that we must suffer loss before we acknowledge gain?

Why is it that we must suffer hurt before we appreciate healing?

Why is it that we must meet with difficulty before we experience understanding?

As we ponder these questions, let us stop to fully grasp the significance that all things are difficult before they are easy . . . that difficulties are stepping stones to success.

And let us forever remember that there is no sunrise without a night.

The Magic of a Snowfall

We crawl sleepily out of bed, stumble to the door, and open it in hopes of finding *positive* headlines in the morning newspaper for a change. But Mother Nature has left us a surprise package. Covering our neighborhood is a beautiful blanket of freshly fallen snow. Our reaction to the gift will depend not only upon our chronological age, but also our age of mind and spirit.

As children, we shout, "Oh, yes!" as we offer praises of joy and thanksgiving for perhaps a free day from school. Our hearts race with enthusiasm as we envision delightful snowball battles with our friends. Our sense of creativity begins to grow as we imagine ways to "dress" our snowman or snowlady that will soon begin taking shape. If we are especially creative, we will make a snowman **and** a snowlady, along with a snowchild or two. We anticipate the fun of lying in the snow and shaping out our snow angels.

You've never made a snow angel?

Oh, it's wonderful fun! Step to a place where the snow has not been disturbed, lie on your back, and move your arms and legs outward in a flying manner. As you leave your angel imprint area, brush the snow back so that all traces of footprints have been removed, and enjoy the sight! Your very own snow angel! And it just *happens* to be your size! But forget trying to make the family pet make his or her own angel. It doesn't work. The animals just do not seem to appreciate the aesthetic beauty of an angel of their own making.

However, as adults, we often see a snowfall in quite a different frame of mind. We moan "Oh, no!" as we offer words of disappointment and gloom for perhaps another frustrating drive to work in the morning rush-hour traffic. Why is it that **we** never get a day free from **work** because of snow? (Unless, of course, we are teachers or the accumulation is up to our shoulders!) **Our** sense of creativity begins to expand as we attempt to think of ways to quickly and efficiently scrape the ice off our frozen automobiles. And if we are especially creative, **we** will make a deal with our children to shovel that white stuff from the driveway. We anticipate the frustration of sitting in traffic and reorganizing our business meeting for which we are now going to be late. **Our** hearts race with dread as we envision being the target of snowballs being hurled at us by neighborhood children.

You've never been late for a meeting?

Oh, it's dreadfully mortifying! Be the last one to enter the room and weakly ask, "Sorry I'm late. Did you see the snow?" We educated adults certainly ask some feeble-minded questions sometimes, don't we? *Did they see the snow!* As if they somehow arrived in that meeting room through interspace travel, completely oblivious to the surrounding whiteout!

We humans, however, are not the only living creatures who relish in a fresh snowfall. Even Mother Nature recognizes the magic of snow as she gives us the beautiful pale gray and brown spotted snow leopard whose *summer* home is at elevations of 13,000 feet or higher.

Or perhaps we have seen the little sparrow-like Snow Bunting. We see this flying friend only when he leaves Canada in the Spring when the North American snowfall is heavy enough to accommodate him. Such a tiny little thing living in such cold climates!

Or perhaps we have seen the Snowy Owl. Although this 20-inch long hunter breeds in the Arctic, he migrates in the winter, sometimes as far south as the Caribbean Sea.

And in the plant world, Mother Nature offers us Snow-on-the-Mountain, the Snowball shrub, and the Snowdrop.

Thus, as we adults consider the many ramifications of fallen snow, we should take a break from the reality of wet boots, slippery roads, slushy sidewalks, snow plows, highway salt, and inconvenience. We should step into the child-like magic of a new snowfall!

The Silence of Snow

A lot of snow fell. Nineteen inches, to be exact. Schools were closed. Malls were closed. Pharmacies were closed. The interstate highways were closed. It seemed that the entire world had stopped in its tracks. No one seemed to appreciate the fact that those beautiful white flakes ranged in size from an eighth of an inch down to the size of the period at the end of this sentence. No one seemed impressed by the fact that the wonderful flakes had begun as dust particles coming together high in the atmosphere. No one really cared that, as these dust particles came in contact with moist air and cold temperatures, they were transformed into microscopic ice crystals that grew larger as they fell closer to the earth.

The 19-inch snowstorm took the city and much of the state by surprise. No one was prepared. Everyone was in a state of panic. No surplus food had been stocked. No preparations had been made for the outdoor pets. No one had filled their automobile tanks with gasoline.

Most people have a love-hate relationship when it comes to snow — especially when a lot of it falls at one time. They love to look at it from their windows, but they hate to deal with it in their driveways and on the streets. They love to see it on their lawns, but they hate to walk through it.

Because the snow had fallen during the night, all of us thought our eyes were playing tricks on us as we looked out the windows for the first time. We stood still with wonderment, yet we wanted to run and shout to everyone, "Look! Look outside."

Being a southern state, Kentucky people were ill-equipped to deal with such amounts of snow. Chains for emergency vehicles could not be located. The snow plows' rubber blades cracked and split, making snow removal almost impossible. Military and four-wheel drive vehicles were the only means of transportation available. But many of the 4-wheel drive vehicles were owned by people who had lived in the South all their lives; the people did not know the mechanics of driving in such accumulated snow. The entire city of nearly a million people was at a complete standstill.

Since I am from the North and possess a deep love for snow, I could hardly wait to get warmly wrapped and head outdoors to enjoy the beauty that Mother Nature had so generously bestowed upon us. I must admit that not all my neighbors felt the enthusiasm I experienced. In fact, I'm not sure *any* of them did. They seemed to feel that some hideous monster had arrived at their doorstep to devour them and their loved ones, though the majority of people could not even *find* their doorsteps because they were buried so deeply in the snow.

I am sure my southern-born neighbors thought this snowfall was an all-time record. Little did they realize the true nature of a real record-breaker. According to the *Guinness Book of World Records*, Silver Lake, Colorado, holds the world record for the greatest amount of snow in a **one-day** period . . . 76 inches in 24 hours on April 15-16, 1921! But northern California holds the distinction of having a record-fall within a **one-week** period . . . 189 inches from February 13-18, 1959! The **one-year** record snow fall belongs to the Mount Rainier Paradise Ranger Station in Washington, where authorities documented 1,222.5 inches from February 18, 1971 - February 18, 1972!

We all have heard it said that no two snowflakes are exactly the same. How do the "experts" know that? Has someone gone out and examined every single snowflake that has ever fallen? Obviously, that would be the only way to know such a fact for certain. A recent news article stated that the estimated number of snowflakes that have ever fallen would total a figure consisting of "1," followed by 36 zeroes. How do they know that, either? Have you ever wondered how they come up with these numbers?

Meanwhile, back to the Kentucky snow . . . My family was the first to venture outdoors that awesome morning. My husband began shoveling so that we could have access to the road. It hadn't occurred to us that no businesses would be open! My children (ages 16 and 20) reveled in the delight of such snowfall. Snowballs began taking shape, and shouts of joy penetrated the quietness. And the family beagle, Spencer, promptly decided he did not care for that white stuff . . . especially considering the fact that he is 13 inches tall at the shoulders, and the snow measured 19 inches. We laughed at the sight of his antics which reminded us of a 25-pound mole tunneling his way to a desired destination. But the poor dog . . . he was so lost and disoriented that he did not know where he wanted to go. He merely stood there, looking pathetically helpless, and using those big brown Beagle eyes to elicit compassion from his family members.

It worked. We tenderly lifted him from the snow and placed him on the porch where he could be "safe" from the elements we were enjoying to the fullest.

Enjoying photography, I snatched the opportunity to head out for some picture-taking. Just the bare essentials, mind you . . . warm clothing, waterproof boots, my camera, two rolls of film, and my whole-hearted enthusiasm. This was the day I had dreamed about many times. But I never expected it in Kentucky. I wanted to be as far away from people as I could get. I desired only the snow, the accompanying stillness, and myself.

Nothing else!

No one else!

Walking was rather difficult in such high snow, but leaving my family and walking down the road was worth every ounce of effort it took to navigate.

The silence was deafening. Its intensity seemed to wrap itself around me and protect me from everything that surrounded my world. I saw no one. I heard nothing. Absolute silence penetrated this glorious gift of snow. The awesome silence seemed to permeate my very soul. Nineteen inches of snow had turned my grass-and-driveway subdivision into a pearly white winter wonderland And it was breath-taking!

As I walked along, I realized that all the shrubs had become snow mounds. Would the snow damage all that growth? Or would it somehow protect it? The holly and magnolia trees struck little resemblance to their identity from the day before. Their branches were so terribly heavy-laden with snow that one thought they would break at any moment. The pine trees were bent into strange positions as the higher branches and tops rested themselves at odd angles to one another.

The precariously balanced snow atop the power lines made one wonder how such accumulation could result from one snowflake at a time. It looked like a high-wire balancing act from Barnum and Bailey. One slip would mean their fall, yet they somehow seemed destined to remain on those wires. One could easily tell the direction from which the snow had blown by watching the telephone poles. One side would be heavily caked with precipitation, while the remaining three sides were clear.

That raises an interesting question. Where does one side stop and another side begin on a round object?

As I drank in the beauty of the snow fields around me, I wondered what elements of life lay buried beneath. Would that life survive, or would it become the beauty's victim? Due to the excessive amount of precipitation in the air, along with the heavy cloud cover, the day was gray and dreary. But even the dreariness possessed a beauty all of its own.

We knew there would be no mail or paper delivery that day. But somehow the activities of the outside world seemed so far-removed and unrelated that they were not all that significant anyway.

The following day was brilliant with sunshine and blue skies, and the former gray snow areas became glistening, sparkling fields of diamonds, the brilliance of which could be matched only by the world's finest gems. The strangely unfamiliar gray world of yesterday became the strangely unfamiliar expression-filled, resplendent world of today with the same snow now sparkling. Two days, so very different, yet so very similar in their own individual glory. Each had a unique gift to present, if only we would take a moment to pause and reflect upon its splendor.

Then Came the Light

As I traveled the interstate highway, I became increasingly aware of the dark, ominous sky. The only shades of color to be seen were grays and blacks. There was a foreboding sense of a storm on the horizon as the air became heavy and full of static. It was almost as though the sky had taken on a personality of dread and sorrow. It seemed to have the countenance of a man deep in thought, pondering what the future held, and greatly concerned about that which awaited him at the next turn.

The clouds were locked into position, and nothing moved. It seemed that the customary expanse of the heavens was on official leave of absence. It appeared that the darkness above was truly coming closer to Earth, making me feel somehow squashed beneath its weight. Being alone in the car intensified the quietness and the apprehension of my surroundings.

As I looked to the four corners of my existence, I saw nothing but the dark clouds that hung immobile above me.

And I began to think about life.

In the periods in life we all experience, circumstances seem to roll in as the heavy clouds and remain locked into position often for a long period of time. We begin to feel the increasing pressure of being crushed under the weight. We attempt to break free, but we continue to feel boxed in and cramped . . . a victim of circumstances.

If life's storm continues, we anxiously search for an escape route, only to discover that no such escape exists. We take on the countenance of a person deep in thought, pondering what the future holds, and concerned about what lies beyond the next turn.

And suddenly the wind began. A seeming complication to an already dreary situation. As the force of nature's howling breath increased, the trees began to bend in the blustering violence.

Leaves that had lain dying since late Fall began dancing on the air currents. Cars began swerving as they encountered the force hitting them from the side, the front, and the rear.

But the wind . . . that force I viewed as my enemy . . . became my friend. In the southwestern sky, as the clouds were forced apart by the wintery blast, graceful silver beams of light poured down from the sky. They were as transparent sterling. Delicate rays of light, trapped above the storm clouds, came racing to Earth, set free by the wind.

And I continued to think about life.

As life's winds force down upon us in our journey through this world, they come not to squash us into oblivion. They come not to crush us into despair. They come not to defeat us into hopelessness.

Rather they come to force apart our self-imposed boundaries and barriers. They come to expose the wondrous rays of sunlight, of moonlight, of starlight that await. They come to remind us that, though temporarily darkened, our skies will once again be bright when comes the light

After the Flood : Part I

I visited my neighboring county today which, along with my own county, had been declared a federal disaster area. The small town had been hit especially hard by the flood waters as the Ohio River overflowed her banks and swelled smaller nearby waterways. As the Salt River could hold no more, she too, overran her banks and spilled into this little town where homes, businesses, and educational facilities suddenly became her victims.

As I slowly drove and walked through the town, the bright sun above warmed me as I tried to comprehend the devastation I saw . . . street signs barely above water level, streets completely immersed, the tops of automobiles hardly visible to the passerby, and residue mud and muck everywhere. I stood quietly, feeling part of a paradox, as I realized the very sun that was warming my body was also creating dazzling sparkles on the very murky water which has been Shepherdsville's vilest enemy in recent days.

And I thought . . . what irony!

One water. Yet two waters.

One beautiful and shining.

The other ugly and dark.

Beauty and the beast . . . standing together.

As I thoughtfully walked down the main street of town, I realized what also caused the eery quiet. Because most of the power in town had been disconnected for safety reasons, the buildings were without light.

And I thought . . . what sadness!

To face the challenge of beginning such a massive clean-up, and facing it in the gloom of darkened, stinking buildings.

And then I saw another source of the quietness. I saw the *absence* of children. Though all county schools were closed, there were no children. Were they still huddled in the shelters with their families? Had their parents sent them to nearby locations to stay with relatives in an attempt to ease the overwhelming shock that children experience at seeing their homes nearly submerged or washed away? Where were the children?

I moved about as unobtrusively as possible. I did not want residents to be aware of my presence. They had been invaded by one stranger. I did not want them to suffer another invasion by another stranger.

I saw the testimonial water marks on homes, some of which had been nearly submerged below the swirling flooding waters. The homes, too, were dark and deserted.

And I saw one of the saddest sights of my life. At one home, where the water was still at basement level, the evacuation of personal possessions had begun. It was not a respectful removal as we would desire for our belongings. But rather men and women had gathered to pull, drag, and push anything from the home they could . . . rugs, padding, furniture, clothing, children's toys, tools . . . everything that bespoke of a normal life for a normal American family.

But nothing was normal now. There was no conversation as the team of neighbors helped. There were no expressions on their faces. Only the body language spoke. It spoke of shock, of hurt, of fear, of uncertainty. And that shock and hurt and fear and uncertainty seemed intensified as a nearby waiting bulldozer made its way toward the home. It scooped its big claw to the earth and . . . completely without thought or feeling . . . tore into the piles of mud-and-water-soaked possessions. Those possessions, representing someone's life, were thrown into an emotionless, waiting truck to be hauled away for disposal. Did the people wonder where their material possessions would go? Or did the shock of the entire flooding nightmare so numb their existence that, at that point in time, they didn't even care? What about the bulldozer operator? What about the truck driver? Did *they* care?

I looked again into the faces of the people whose home . . . and perhaps *hearts* . . . were being emptied. The presence of utter despair radiated from their being.

I stood almost reverently as I watched this event unfold before my eyes. I was trying, as best I could, to show respect for the pain and trauma these people were experiencing. I tried to place myself in their position, to feel their heartache, but I failed miserably. I could not imagine the sense of total loss and confusion one must feel under such circumstances.

Since I was on higher ground, I walked down the road a little further. Again, no children. No pets. No adults. Another house in particular, sitting in isolation among many, offered no sign of life. Then I realized what had attracted my attention to this piece of property.

Sitting near the mailbox was a child's scooter. A scooter that was covered with mud and filth. A scooter that was twisted and bent. A scooter that should have been under the feet of a child playing in the warmth of spring sunlight . . . not sitting silently alone as a testimony to the ravaged evidence of nature's destructive force.

I stood at the open cafeteria door of the school where I taught Alternative Education students for two years. From there, I saw the muddy water marks on the walls nearly six feet from the floor. I saw the totally destroyed desks, chairs, and tables we see each day in schools. Had it been piled into the cafeteria in an attempt to save it on higher ground? Had it been washed there by the force of the raging water? Or had the clean-up begun, and it was awaiting its turn, too, for the dump truck?

How many dump trunks would leave this little town . . . dump trucks filled with tears and turmoil? With darkness and despair? With trinkets and treasures? With dreams and dread? With memory-filled yesterdays and hope-filled tomorrows?

And the people . . . what about the people? What will they do *today?*

After the Flood: Part II

I went into the small flooded town again. I didn't want to see the despair again, but something kept pulling me back . . . a tugging that wouldn't let go.

It had only been two days since I first visited, but I could quickly see that the water had receded somewhat. The majority of the city was still without power, and that somehow made the whole scene even more intense. Two days before, the sun had been shining, and I think that helped to lift spirits a little . . . perhaps very little, but at such a traumatic time, every positive aspect helps.

But on this day the town looked even more disheartening, the people more cast down, the body language more hopeless. For at two o'clock in the afternoon, the skies were gray and foreboding, and it was raining. The bitter pain of falling water had hit again.

The few people I saw simply stood in disbelief as they looked either toward the sky or straight ahead. But I sensed they were not truly seeing anything . . . or feeling anything. Their countenances radiated numbness. Their movements were slow, as though shoved into neutral by an innate sense of survival.

I went back to the school where I had taught for two years and walked through muddy sludge to the front of the building. I wiped the dried mud from the outside of the ground level window to my old classroom so I could see inside. I knew it would not be a pretty sight, but I was not prepared for what I saw. I was looking at what had formerly been my classroom. But it did not resemble my room in the least. It did not resemble *any* classroom.

File cabinet drawers were separated from their frames. Muddied textbooks lay everywhere. Files, folders of curriculum, and student desks were strewn about the room in total chaos as though an inhuman giant of anger and destruction had swept through the interior. The old wooden teacher's desk sat entombed in mud. Maps and charts on the walls hung in wet crumples. The mud stains on the walls told me that the water level had reached two inches above the top of the four-drawer metal filing cabinets, and the receding water had left them caked in an inch of mud.

It was not my classroom. It had not been my classroom for two years. But my friend had been teaching in that room since I left. Perhaps that is why I still had a kinship to it.

As I stood looking at the debris-cluttered interior and mud-soaked interior and contents, I realized what frustration I was feeling. For I had written much of the curriculum that now lay in soaked piles of useless trash. I felt a deep sense of hurt . . . and anger . . . a sense of having been violated by the rampaging Salt River.

I felt anxiety when I remembered the orderliness and physical attractiveness that represented my classroom. It had always been bright and colorful and cheerful. I wanted that as much for myself as for my students. We had to spend many hours a day there, and I wanted that room to be a pleasant experience for all concerned.

But there was nothing orderly or attractive or cheerful about that room. It was dark and cold and filthy and deathly quiet. How many teachers' and students' possessions were destroyed beyond use . . . or gone, never to be seen again?

I also felt a deep sense of helplessness . . . realizing that we humans (with all of our intelligence, education, sophistication, and technology) can do little in the face of a natural disaster.

Perhaps, in that moment of inner turmoil I was feeling . . . perhaps I had a tiny vestige of understanding of what the victims of Mother Nature were experiencing in that small town. The numbness, the devastation, the hurt, the frustration, and anger . . . all the emotions we cannot understand until we have experienced them first hand.

. . . about

ANIMAL NATURE

Kitty Claws and Puppy Paws

There is a four-legged creature who has lived at our house for the last 8 years who will steal your heart with his big brown eyes, his long floppy ears, and his almost-human expressive face. As he listens to your voice, his head turns from side to side as though he were completely understanding all that you have to say. He is Spencer, the family Beagle.

Spencer was a twelfth-birthday present for our son, Mark, and it was Mark's privilege to name him. We thought the name *Spencer* was a rather sophisticated name for such a breed of dog, but the little puppy's fate had been determined. He was going to be named Spencer, and that was the end of the discussion.

Several months after the pooch came into our family, a neighborhood cat wandered by (looking as though it were starved both for food and affection). Since more than one member of my family has an allergy to cats, we knew this feline would not be staying long. But we took pity on the poor thing and let it in the house for a few minutes while we treated it to a pan of milk on the kitchen floor. We knew the cat's name was Blackie, which was most appropriate, since he was completely black . . . not a white hair anyplace on his body that we could see.

Now I had never been around cats and knew nothing of their behavior. Thus, when the pan of milk was served to Blackie, I was surprised to see him sit down to drink it. After all, the dogs my father had raised never sat down to drink. And neither had any of my own dogs. Thus, I decided that this was yet another difference between cats and dogs.

Quietly and without ceremony, Blackie began to enjoy his milk treat, sitting with his back to all of us.

All the family members were watching the cat lap up the milk, almost as a vacuum sweeper pulls in dirt. That milk was disappearing **fast**! And as the milk began to disappear, the cat's tail began twitching. I have learned since that time that a cat's twitching tail under such circumstances generally means contentment. But I did not know that little tidbit of information at the time, however.

I realized I was not the only one watching the cat's tail. Spencer was watching it also. With each twitch of that little black tail, Spencer watched more intently. As his head began to cock from side to side, he s-l-o-w-l-y crept forward two or three steps.

He stopped dead in his tracks. He didn't move for the longest time. And all the while, the cat continued to lap up his milk, enjoying every drop. Suddenly, with the speed of lightning, Spencer leaped on that poor cat's tail with all the enthusiasm his puppyhood could muster. He had found a new toy! And it moved!

But Blackie had other ideas! He did not intend to be *anyone's* plaything!

Quick as a flash, that cat leaped from the floor, spun around, and attacked poor Spencer without mercy.

Faster than the eye could count, that cat's paw smacked the poor pup repeatedly in the nose. Between the cat's hissing and the pup's screeching, we didn't know whether to laugh or cry. It was a true comedy/tragedy being played out in real life . . . right in the middle of our kitchen floor.

By this time, both animals were on the slick linoleum floor trying desperately to escape each other, yet neither going anywhere. There was the slipping and sliding of kitty feet and doggie paws. After what seemed to be an interminable period of time (especially for the two animals, I'm sure), each managed to escape to his own corner of the kitchen. The cat headed toward the living room, while the pup headed for the family room.

Totally opposite directions!

But who could blame them?

Both of them must have felt as if their world had collapsed around them, snaring them into the terrified scenario from which each had miraculously escaped. Neither animal had been seriously injured.

But poor Blackie . . . he sat licking his tail, ever watchful of Spencer.

And poor Spencer . . . he sat *attempting* to lick the drops of blood from his nose, ever watchful of Blackie.

Since the cat was not ours to begin with, he was promptly removed from the house. We did not want more damage from his teeth and claws although we could not blame him for his reaction to the pup. I am sure it was quite a normal response for a cat, considering the circumstances.

I have decided that the entire incident was truly traumatic for Spencer. The poor dog was not his usual self for **days!** Every time he would approach the kitchen, or *any* corner around which he could not see, he would pause, develop a look of consternation on his face, then proceed cautiously to his destination.

In the months and years that followed, Blackie and Spencer came in contact with each on several occasions. And I am convinced that at least *some* animals have very long and accurate memories. For on every occasion that these two animals met, they cut each other a W - I - D - E path! A lesson bitterly learned, but learned nonetheless.

Three Raccoons and an Apple Tree

We have been fortunate to have a variety of animals on our property, but perhaps the funniest of all was a family of three young raccoons. As we watched their antics through the kitchen window, we realized we could be watching three brothers, three sisters, two brothers and a sister, or two sisters and a brother. We also realized that determining the gender of the three playful souls really didn't matter.

We were mesmerized by the raccoons' ringed tails, erect ears, and pointed snouts. But, of course, we could hardly look away from those undescribably cute "masked" faces. Were those actual *expressions* we saw? Researchers tell us that raccoons make good pets when they are young. Their winsome personalities and sense of curiosity intrigue even the most sophisticated adults, but by the time they are one year old, the animals can be easily angered and tend to bite their owners.

While we were in the back yard one day, we were watching these lively critters in their natural habitat, and we had no desire to capture them. The three of them raced around the tree, up the tree, down the tree, and we were amazed that they managed *not* to collide with each other during their hectic racing. I wonder if they momentarily ever forgot whether they were racing **up** the tree or **down** the tree? Do animals ever forget things like that?

As the game of "catchers" continued, the raccoons rarely stopped to catch their breath. They seemed oblivious to the fact that they were playing in the midst of humans' back yard. Perhaps, because we never bother the animals, they felt the freedom and security to entertain us. We have often seen possums, ground hogs, squirrels, and chipmunks on our property. We have also seen two or three skunks, one red fox, a deer, and one cow. Since our property has a "park" atmosphere, the cow truly seemed out of place. We learned that she had "escaped" from her owner several properties away and apparently decided to take a scenic tour of the neighborhood.

But raccoons? We had never observed raccoons on the property before, and we were certainly enjoying their performance. As our fascination with them increased, we crept quietly and slowly nearer, not wanting to frighten them. We merely wanted a better view.

Their funny shenanigans continued until we were almost directly under them. Then suddenly they stopped.

We were afraid we had gotten too close.

We were afraid they would run, and we would never see them again.

Run . . . they didn't.

Stay . . . they did!

But the situation was suddenly reversed.

We, the *observers*, were now the *observed*.

The raccoons stopped their racing as each took his or her rightful position somewhere in the tree. Each found a branch to sit upon. But their position quickly changed from **sitting** to **hanging.** As their paws grasped the branches, the raccoons twisted and turned their bodies in various directions to watch us intensely as we sat motionless on the ground. Their contorted positions and their inquisitive faces amused us to such a degree that it was difficult to keep from laughing out loud. But we did not want to do anything to frighten them away, so we continued our silent watch.

Finally, the critters must have decided that watching those boring humans doing nothing but sitting quietly on the ground was a waste of their precious time. They quickly changed into race mode again as they scampered down the tree and into the surrounding landscape.

I wonder . . . can raccoons think? Did they realize we would never harm them? Did they realize how much we enjoyed them? And after they arrived home for the evening, did they have a family discussion about those crazy humans sitting on the ground looking up into the tree?

Our day had been made complete by three raccoons and an apple tree.

Spencer and Hamlet

We often joke about our home being Heizer's Zoo. For over the years, we have cared for box turtles, snapping turtles, rabbits, one field mouse, fishing worms, dogs, cats, frogs, guinea pigs, tropical fish, and one horse. All of them lived inside **except** the cats and the horse. The cats because of family allergies . . . the horse because of size. Although, if my daughter had had her way, the horse would have lived in her bedroom.

But the animal population at the Heizer Zoo is somewhat small at the moment . . . only a 30-pound Beagle who answers to the name of Spencer, and a one-pound guinea pig appropriately named Hamlet.

Spencer and Hamlet entertained themselves today. They also entertained *us*. And they reminded us of two valuable lessons in life. It is quite a sight to watch a four-legged Beagle leisurely stroll through the hall while a four-legged guinea pig races along to keep ahead of his friend. Since Hamlet's legs are somewhat shorter than Spencer's, he is at a distinct disadvantage in the daily marathons. But while Hamlet is short on legs, he is long on spirit. And so the sprints continue.

Up the hall. And down the hall. And up the hall. And down the hall. Back and forth they go. Covering the same piece of territory again and again, yet not tiring of the repeated scenery. Spencer leisurely walking. Hamlet scampering for all he's worth as fast as his little legs will carry him. Each keeping an eye on the other.

What do they think as they continue this ritual? Do they have any thoughts? Or do they merely engage into automatic pilot? We believe animals can think, but to what degree? Obviously, we will never know for certain, for we have heard of no animal who has spoken to us and *told* us what he thinks.

But back to the races . . . on they go, racking up miles on their legs, keeping their cardiovascular systems fit through proper exercise, and thoroughly enjoying each other's company. They have very little in common. One likes to run through the woods; the other likes to scamper on the carpet. One likes to eat pizza; the other enjoys lettuce. One barks; the other squeaks. One drinks water from a metal bowl; the other drinks from a plastic water bottle. One chews; the other nibbles. One sleeps on a soft blanket; the other sleeps in cedar shavings.

Yet in spite of all their differences, they take pleasure in one other's presence. They find the arrangement to be mutually satisfying.

LESSON ONE was about to be driven home.

The guinea pig does not try to change Spencer, and Spencer does not attempt to make Hamlet see the world through the eyes of a Beagle. There are no arguments as to which is preferred sleeping material . . . a blanket or cedar shavings. There are no discussions as to whether pizza or lettuce is a better food. There are no debates focusing upon the topic of which turf (woods or carpet) makes the better race track. Each enjoys the world from his own perspective.

Suddenly the racing stops. Hamlet turns and faces Spencer (who must look like the jolly black, brown, and white giant). Neither of them moves for the longest time. Whose **courage** or **curiosity** will get the best of him first? Will it be the Beagle? Or will it be the guinea pig? My money is on the guinea pig. The Beagle is seven years old. He has learned the value of patience. The guinea pig is only three months old, and he is not so wise.

They are nose-to-nose. Spencer's big nose. Hamlet's little nose. Spencer sits down, lowers his head, and watches his friend with the expressive brown eyes and droopy ears that only a Beagle can muster. Surely Hamlet will run. He is David facing Goliath.

But not this feisty little guinea pig. He has no intention of running. Quick as a flash, Hamlet licks Spencer's big black nose with his own tiny little pink tongue. And quick as *another* flash, Spencer jumps back, taken completely off guard by his little friend's gesture. LESSON TWO was about to be reinforced.

Goliath is defeated again. And David is the victor again!

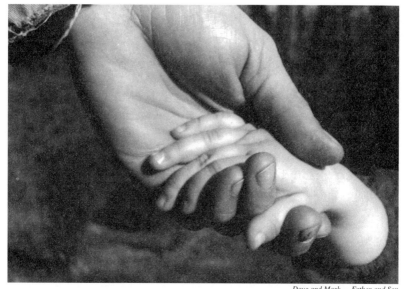

Dave and Mark — Father and Son

◆ ◆ ◆ about

HUMAN NATURE

Opportunity Knocks;
It Doesn't Break Down the Door

Jim Corbett, the former world's heavyweight boxing champion, often told the story of the day he was out jogging for an upcoming fight. As he continued his run, he came upon a man who was fishing. It was time in his workout for a short break, so Corbett decided to stop and watch the man for a while.

Shortly the man began pulling and tugging at his line and quickly pulled in a large trout. The fisherman examined his catch closely, then tossed it back into the water. After a few more moments, the man pulled in a large perch, examined it closely, and threw it back in also. Before long, the old fisherman brought in a small trout. He examined it closely, put it in his basket, and prepared to leave.

Corbett's curiosity peaked, and he asked the old man why he had thrown the two larger fish back, yet kept the small one. The fisherman replied, "Small frying pan."

We laugh at such foolishness, yet we must ask ourselves if we, too, do not pass by larger opportunities for fear of not being capable of handling them. We jump to the conclusion that we are not up to the task, that somehow we lack whatever it would require to complete the chore. We look at other individuals' accomplishments and think that "lady luck" was good to them.

Max O'Rell once observed,

"Luck means the hardships and privations which you have not hesitated to endure; the long nights you have devoted to work. Luck means the appointments you have never failed to keep; the trains you have never failed to catch."

We speak of self-made men, yet we must wonder if there truly are such creatures. Such individuals, in my opinion, simply watch their world closely, seize the opportunities that come their way, and then make use of such opportunities.

Is a sense of uncertainty present in such circumstances? Certainly. Yet most of life is an uncertainty. There are no written guarantees of what will come tomorrow. We frequently give credit to others' successes by concentrating upon their great qualities and feel that we, ourselves, do not possess such qualities. We must remember, however, that the greatest of qualities are of no consequence if we do not utilize them!

Perhaps the mark of successful individuals is in those who realize the importance of setting goals for themselves so that they may create a time line of achievements. For if we do not set goals, how will we ever know if we have achieved them? We oftentimes fail because of the power of our minds.

We are told by elephant trainers that the huge beasts can be taught to stay by their stake in the ground, held only with a small rope. That is, however, *after* they have been trained by being held in place with chains they *cannot* break. They are held in place not by the power of the rope. Not by the power of the trainer. Not by the power of the stake.

Rather, they are held in place by their own mentality.

Their huge bulk could easily snap the small ropes, but because they **believe** they cannot escape, they **do** not.

Our world is full of instances where men, women, children, and even animals have accomplished tasks thought by everyone around them to be impossible.

For example, Hollywood actor Tom Cruise suffered from dyslexia so badly that, when he first began his acting career, he hired someone to repeatedly read the scripts to him until he memorized them. Or he listened to tapes of the scripts in order to memorize them.

Woodrow Wilson, as a young boy of nine, did not know the letters of the alphabet. He finally learned to read at age 11. The adults in his world thought he was dull and backward. But later in life he entered Princeton University where he received average grades. Still later in life, he became President of the United States.

Winston Churchill had much difficulty in school, yet became a national leader and the Prime Minister of England.

There was another boy who, at age four, still could not talk. He could not read until he was nine years old. His teachers believed that he was mentally slow, withdrawn, and a daydreamer. He desperately wanted to attend college but failed the entrance exams. He finally passed the exams after spending a full year preparing for them. He was dismissed from his first three teaching positions, and later became a patent clerk. Who was this poor individual who would most likely never contribute much to society? Albert Einstein . . . one of the greatest scientists of all times. His theory of relativity revolutionized the manner in which scientists around the world viewed time, space, motions, mass, and gravity.

One final example is the lowly bumble bee. According to the laws of aerodynamics, our bee friend cannot fly. But no one ever told him he could not fly

. . . and so he does.

And what of us? Are we listening and watching for opportunity to knock, or are we waiting for it to break down the door?

Someone once said,

Four things come not back:

The spoken word; The sped arrow;

Time past; And the neglected opportunity.

All of us must admit that we have permitted opportunities (perhaps golden opportunities) to slip through our fingers at one time or another. But we can also take *this* opportunity to confirm within ourselves that we will, from this time forward, be more vigilant to take notice of those occasions that come to all of us, at one time or another.

Are we willing to be persistent in taking risks?

Mud Puddles or Wading Pools

We all have heard the story of the man who said his glass was half empty, while his friend said that his glass was half full. It is simply a matter of perception . . . or perhaps we should use the word *attitude*. It is a rather small word with only 8 letters. But it is a word that is full of power, for it is our manner of acting, feeling, or thinking that shows our disposition, opinion, or mental mindset.

Our attitude allows us to take a chance, risk the unknown, step into the unfamiliar, and rise above the odds against us and achieve tasks we never thought possible. **OR** our attitude allows us to stay in our familiar routine, never venturing into strange waters, sink into doom and despair, and spend our lives contemplating the "what if's" that we never had the courage to attempt.

Our path in life is not determined by the external elements surrounding us . . . the people, the circumstances, and the conditions that exist in our world. Our path in life is determined by the internal workings of ourselves . . . our disposition, our habits, our sentiments, and our outlook that exist within our hearts and spirits.

Many years ago two competing shoe salesmen arrived at about the same time in Africa. Their job was to develop the consumer market for their respective companies. Wanting to create this market in the most needy area, both men headed for the innermost regions of the continent. After several weeks, one of the men telephoned his company. He was frustrated, disappointed, and returning home on the next boat. There are no sales opportunities here," he said. "The natives don't wear shoes."

At about the same time, the other salesman excitedly sent a telegram to his company. "Quick . . . send hundreds of pairs of shoes in all sizes, styles, and colors. The people here have no shoes."

Two individuals finding themselves in the same circumstances. One chooses to walk away from his in a negative and defeatist attitude, balking at the current situation, resistive to any possible change. The other, seeing the positive potential, capitalized on his circumstances, assured and confident that he could change the status quo. Each man had the freedom to choose. And each man lived with the results of his choice.

We have the power to achieve things we never dreamed of, do things we never thought we could. There are few limitations in what we can achieve except for the limitations we place upon ourselves within our own mind. We cannot think we *can't*. We must think we *can.*

Do we ever stop to think about who we really are? We must remember that it is our actions and attitudes when we are on our own that reflect who and what we really are. Yet as we see our true selves in our "alone" times, we must also realize that our attitude as an individual usually determines the attitude of those around us. Can we recall a time when a down-in-the-mouth person entered our midst, and before long, everyone involved was of the same attitude? On the other hand, can we recall a time when a happy, chipper soul entered our midst, and before long, everyone seemed to be feeling better?

Coincidence? No.

Contagious attitude? Yes.

The pessimists will appraise their circumstances, consider the alternatives, and realize the number of things that could go wrong. They know within their hearts that Murphy's law that states, "If things can go wrong, they will" is absolute truth. Thus they decide that such risks are not worth the opportunities.

The optimists will appraise their circumstances, consider the alternatives, and see the number of gains that could be realized from their endeavor. They, too, know that Murphy's law exists. Yet, in spite of Murphy, they decide that such opportunities are, indeed, worth the risks.

Phillips Brooks, an American clergyman and bishop, is most likely remembered for his Christmas carol "O Little Town of Bethlehem." But Brooks also believed that life is in our blood and never will be still. He continues on to say, "It will be a sad day for individuals when they become contented with the thoughts they are thinking and the deeds they are doing . . . where there is not forever beating at the doors of their souls some great desire to do something larger. Something they know they were meant and made to do."

Any endeavor has its risks. But we must always remind ourselves that those who try to do something . . . and *fail* . . . are infinitely better off than those who try to do nothing . . . and *succeed*. For as the poet James Russell Lowell reminded us, "Not failure, but low aim, is the crime."

Sympathy or Compassion

It would probably be safe to say that all humans have felt pity or sympathy for someone or something at one point or another in their lives. To experience pity or sympathy, one must feel deep sorrow or a sameness of feelings for another's suffering or misfortune.

As we read or hear of tragedies in the national media, our hearts go out to the individuals who have experienced great trauma or loss. We may feel great sorrow for the victims of earthquakes, tornados, hurricanes, and floods. We will, perhaps, experience intense feelings of sadness when learning of a family losing all their material possessions or a beloved pet or, especially, a loved one in a fiery explosion.

We may find ourselves concerned over the families of victims who have perished as the result of a mine explosion or bridge collapse or air disaster. We may even pause for a moment and give thanks for our own children when hearing of a family who has been devastated by the loss of a child in a terrible accident. We pause momentarily to meditate upon the heartache involved in such human tragedies, but we quickly resume our daily routine with a nominal amount of afterthought.

But compassion . . . that takes us to a deeper level of involvement. An involvement that produces commitment. **Compassion** is defined in *Webster's New World Dictionary* as "sorrow for the sufferings of others, accompanied by an urge to help."

The story is often told of a poor old farmer in serious trouble near the town of Rochdale, England. A local mill owner was walking up the hill from town one day when he passed upon the old farmer and his horse. The animal had stumbled into a gopher hole and broken its leg. Knowing the animal could not be saved, the farmer was overcome both by the grief for his soon-to-be-destroyed horse *and* his desperate financial situation, made even worse by this recent accident.

Friends and neighbors began gathering around the old farmer, all expressing their sorrow at the old man's great loss. The mill owner removed his hat, placed five pounds in it and announced to those standing nearby, "I am sorry five pounds for our neighbor. How sorry are you?"

The miller passed the hat and collected enough money for the poor old farmer to buy another horse.

The friends and neighbors were expressing their pity and sympathy. The miller was expressing true compassion, for he not only *felt* . . . he *helped.* He was willing to add hands and feet to his heart.

We sometimes forget that true compassion comes in all sizes, shapes, and colors. We oftentimes mistakenly believe that compassion and education are somehow linked, and that lacking the one means lacking the other. We are misled by appearances.

A missionary was leading an expedition of white men to the Negrito people of the Philippines . . . an undernourished race of people who were known for their harmlessness and gentle spirit. The trek involved a long upward mountain climb, with the temperature nearing 125 degrees. The heat was causing the expedition members extreme discomfort. As the noon hour approached, the expedition members spread lunch for themselves under the trees in an attempt to escape the searing midday heat that was causing the members difficulty in breathing.

As they began eating, a hideously sore-ridden old Negrito man approached the group and watched as they ate. A newspaper man traveling with the group observed, "There is the most hideous human being I have ever seen. I have traveled in South

America, Africa, and all over the South Seas, and I have never seen a human being nearer an animal than that old beast."

Suddenly the old man disappeared but shortly returned, accompanied by other members of his race. He had noticed that one of the expedition members was ill; he motioned for the member to lie down. The old Negrito then provided a huge palm leaf as a fan and a bamboo cup of fresh spring water for the ailing man to drink. All the while, the old man spoke not a word.

After the white men finished their lunch, they offered the old man a sandwich. All the men present could see the hunger in the old Negrito's eyes, and they were astonished as they witnessed the old man giving his food to a mother and her malnourished child. Upon seeing his generosity, the expedition leader offered the old man another sandwich. He turned toward his people and offered the nourishment to a timid old woman. When offered yet another sandwich, the old man gave it to another hungry old man.

The old man's generosity touched the hearts of the expedition members. They continued to offer him food . . . all of which he gave to the starving group that had accompanied him. Only when all of his people had been fed did the Negrito take food for himself.

The expedition members sat in stunned silence as they observed the tender compassion and love shown by this starving, uneducated, dirty, sore-ridden old man. The Caucasians, in all of their educated intelligence, had only hours before decided that the old man was "a beast nearer an animal" than anything they had ever seen!

Thus, as we look in the world around us and learn of hurting people on all sides, will we feel with simply our hearts, or will we allow those feelings to spread to our hands and our feet? Are we willing to make the commitment? Although we cannot save the world, will we be willing to begin where we are and strive to make a difference there? Or will we think about these things for a while but quickly become absorbed again in our own little world?

The question is not whether we will share of our finances or our talents or our time. The question is . . . will we give of ourselves?

Frogs in the Water

As the word *animal* comes to mind, all of us could quickly name our favorite creatures who either walk, crawl, fly, or swim. We may think of the largest land animal, the elephant. Or we may think of the largest sea animal, the blue whale, which is longer than eight elephants standing in a row. Or we may think of the giraffe, the tallest of all animals. Bird lovers may think of the smallest of their species, the hummingbird, which can fly straight up into the air like a helicopter.

The adult mayfly will live only from a few hours to a few days, while the giant tortoise usually lives more than 100 years. Or, if we have a special fondness for ears, we may think of the African elephant, whose ears generally measure 4 feet across. Or if we like to look at eyes, we may think of the two land animals known especially for the size of their eyes . . . the horse and the ostrich. Their eyes are normally one and a half times as large as a human's eyes.

As we look to the animal kingdom to learn our lessons from nature, we generally think in terms of the "higher intelligence" animals such as apes and monkeys, the dolphins and whales, the elephants and horses.

Perhaps something we do *not* realize is that the pig is the best problem-solver of all hoofed animals.

Many years ago, scientists conducted a series of experiments from which they gained insight not only into animal behavior but also into human behavior. In the laboratory, Frog A was dropped into a beaker of boiling water. He immediately leaped out of the water, thereby saving himself from certain death. Frog B was also placed in a beaker of water, but the water was the same temperature as the frog's body temperature. A small flame was placed under the beaker, and it slowly but steadily increased the water's temperature.

The frog died within the hour.

The scientists concluded that the second frog died because he was unaware of the gradually rising temperature.

If we choose to do so, we can learn a valuable lesson from those two frogs. The majority of us could easily identify with Frog A whose consciousness of his surroundings and its immediate change alerted the creature to self-disaster. His survival instincts went into over-drive, and he escaped calamity.

Then there is Frog B . . . poor soul . . . who, because of his inattentiveness to a changing environment, perished. Not many of us humans would care to identify ourselves with the second frog. We would tend to label him *stupid, dense, mentally defective*, or *brainless*. After all, the dumb frog sat in that water until he literally "cooked to death." Only a moron would do something as simple-minded as that.

But wait a minute! Have we, also, suddenly awakened to the reality of our circumstances, only to discover that we are in the middle of a catastrophic calamity from which we **may** not escape? Have we ever found ourselves in a disastrous mess simply because we did not heed the slowly emerging danger signals that were all about us?

If we have found ourselves in such a dilemma, was it because we simply did not care about the consequences? Or was it because we thought we could somehow escape the inevitable . . . that the laws that governed other people's behavior did not apply to us?

When we realized our water was boiling, did we chalk it up to ignorance? Or perhaps arrogance?

Or does it really matter *what* label we hung on it?

The major point of consideration is that we were surrounded by evidence, yet we did not take necessary steps to prevent our being cooked to death.

The story is told of a camel who, during a cold, windy night in the desert, pushed his nose into the tent of his Arabic master. The creature, cold and shivering, asked, "It is so cold out tonight, do you mind if I place just my nose in your tent?"

The Arab could see no harm in the request, granted the camel's wish, and promptly went back to sleep. But later into the night, the Arab awakened and realized that his camel had also placed his head, neck, and shoulders in the tent. The beast pleaded his case, causing the Arab to feel such pity that he allowed the animal to put his forelegs into the tent also.

Still, the camel was not satisfied and pleaded with his master to allow him to fully sleep in the tent with him. The Arab was a kind soul, could see no harm in the request, and granted his permission.

As dawn broke over the horizon, the Arab awakened to find himself stiff and shivering from cold **and** covered with blowing desert sand. Not understanding his present condition, he arose to find himself outside the tent.

The camel was sleeping comfortably and peacefully inside.

Yet another lesson in our need to be quite conscious of our changing environment.

Will we learn from the compassionate, yet gullible, Arab?

Will we learn from the frogs in the water?

Lonely in the Crowd

I have been thinking a lot lately about today's society.

The careless attitude we demonstrate to our children.

The neglectful disrespect we show our elders.

The hectic pace at which we move.

The thoughtless way we abuse our resources.

The self-serving attitude we have toward nature.

The unobserved path we take through life.

I have recently been reading about the Lakota (Sioux) Indians and their love of nature, and I believe all races could learn many lessons from our Native Americans and their shared reverence for all aspects of nature. They understood the principle of working *with* the land, and that taking *from* the land meant also giving *to* the land. The Lakotas, however, had an especially deep love of nature. In a book titled ***Land of the Spotted Eagle*** (1933), Luther Standing Bear gives a detailed account of what a true love of nature can do for the human spirit.

Standing Bear, born in the mid 1860s (sent to an Indian school in Pennsylvania, and returned to his tribe at the age of 16) begins by saying, "Everywhere there was life. Even without human companionship one was never alone." Yet near the end of his life as he returned to his tribe after an absence of many years, Standing Bear was disheartened to see how poverty-stricken and demoralized his people had become as a result of being forced to live on a reservation.

As we travel back in time, we see the *original* Americans learning to live in a natural environment where strong communal ties were valued and practiced. They cared deeply for one another and met the needs of others within their group, for they realized that their strength and survival lay in the unity of body and spirit.

But as commerce and commercial trade made their inroads into human economy, those communal ties were laid aside in favor of personal recognition and gain. As such goals were reached, independence and freedom began its reign. And with that independence and freedom came increased isolation and loneliness. Gone were the days of a community taking pride in its work. Gone were the days of a family sensing joy in its creative crafts. *Individuality* was the name of the new game.

When the Native Americans' life of rivers and animals and mountains and plants gave way to the modern American society of fiberglass and synthetic materials and plastic, individuals became alienated from themselves. They were suddenly attempting to fit into a world of machinery and technology rather than continuing to be an integral part of the natural world around them. And with this alienation came an emptiness and loneliness that manifests itself in an inability to give and receive satisfying and mature love. We cannot freely give of ourselves to others *or* to our world when we are constantly reminded to put "Number One" first.

As we have become educated, sophisticated, and technologically advanced, we have removed ourselves from nature and elevated ourselves above it. We have taken from nature that which we wanted, removed that which was inconvenient to our "new and improved" way of life. We destroyed that which was momentarily useless (we thought).

Today's nature lover is seen as one who delights in the natural world almost as an unnecessary sideline or pastime compared to a more serious vocation of industry and finance and corporate America. Yet if this love is so superficial or unimportant to the true quality of life, why is it that increased numbers of individuals are attempting to escape the stress and strain of today's world by retreating to the lakes for fishing, the woods for hiking, and the parks for camping? Why is it that the increased numbers of yearly visitors to our national parks are threatening the very survival of their plants and animals?

Is there not something deep in all of us that yearns for a life of communion with nature? Do we not hear a cry within our hearts that calls for a periodic release from our mechanical and technical world?

And when we find those individuals who possess that strong passion for nature, do we not assume that they are attempting to fill a void created by a lack or loss of relationships? Do we not assume they are *substituting* one thing for another?

We watch with delight as animals carry out their characteristic antics. We breathe in the wonderful aromas after a rain. We listen to the deafening quietness after a snowfall. We watch the spectacular beauty of a sunset and feel that peace within ourselves that calms and refreshes us. No machines. No electrical gadgets. No battery-operated gizmos. Only ourselves and nature at its finest!

However, few of us rise early enough to take the time to soak in the glorious sunrise that begins many of our days. Standing Bear explains that his people would rise before dawn to begin yet another 24-hour segment of their lives. However, at the moment when the sun rose from its bed on the horizon, his people would stop their work . . . would stop their talk . . . and quietly stand in thoughtful meditation to appreciate the beginning of another brand new day they had been given. It was considered a sacred time when all people . . . men, women, and children . . . would pause and give thanks for the sun and its life-giving rays.

Standing Bear believed, "Everything around . . . was a source of knowledge and inspiration. The world was a library and its books were the stones, leaves, brooks, birds, and animals that shared (alike with us) the storms and blessings of earth." Indian children were taught to observe the animals and to apply their behavior to human need and life. Indian children were stimulated by observing, and taking part in, nature at its very best *and* its very worst. Today's children are stimulated by ugly cartoons on television and violence and noise and self-wants and peer pressure.

Indian children understood their world and spent their days grasping their role in cooperating with nature. Today's children are grasping at straws in attempt to discover *who* they are, *what* they are, and *why* they are!

During the 1960s, John Lennon and Paul McCartney wrote a song in which they asked where all the lonely people were coming from. We could very well ask that same question now. In today's mass population, in today's busy world of men and machines, in today's world of materialistic wealth, in today's world of cheering crowds . . . where *are* all the lonely people coming from?

Searching for the Beauty,
or Searching for the Beautiful

In today's glamour-crazed world, we spend fortunes in money, time, and energy searching for beauty. We contemplate nips, tucks, suctions, lifts, reductions, and implants . . . all in the name of beauty. We have forgotten Plato's reminder, "Beauty of style and harmony and grace depend on simplicity." We are madly chasing that elusive butterfly which taunts us to enhance the outer self in attempting the make the inner self more pleasing. We are driven to frustration and exhaustion trying to find that complex structure . . . whether it be physical, intellectual, or spiritual . . . that we desire in an attempt to set ourselves above the crowd.

In our mad frenzy to *be* the best, *have* the best, and *buy* the best, we have lost sight of what is truly important. The advertising industry uses beauty to sell everything from Alcohol to Zinc oxide, all the while telling us to "Go ahead. Splurge. You're worth it." George Bancroft, the 19th century American historian, diplomat, and teacher held the basic affirmation, "Beauty, like truth and justice, lives within us; like virtue and like moral law, true beauty is a companion of the soul."

We buy our daughters dolls with hour-glass figures, glamorous hair styles, and mountainous wardrobes of clothing. We buy them children's cosmetic cases so they can make themselves "beautiful."

We buy our sons moving figures of soldiers and athletes that are laden with brawn and princely good looks.

What would happen if, suddenly upon our television screen, there appeared a commercial for moral character, mature disposition, congenial personality, and benevolent and forgiving attitudes? Would anyone continue watching, or would everyone make their mad dash to the refrigerator, feeling that such attributes are obsolete and have no real value in today's society?

Have we so emphasized the external appearance that we have forgotten the true value of the individual? Have we forgotten how to look past the outer human, so that we may examine and regard the inner being? How many inner treasures of humanity we overlook in others because we do not take time to go beyond the outer layer of appearance!

Francis Bacon, the English philosopher and statesman who lived during the late 1500s and early 1600s, phrased it so aptly when he stated, "The best part of beauty is that which no picture can express." Perhaps you know someone today who may not score high on the "Richter scale for looks" but who has an inner beauty that transcends popular definition. Take time right now to drop that individual a written word of encouragement or praise. Perhaps it could be a note of thanks, simply expressing your appreciation for *who* and *what* that person is.

I attended school with a girl who undoubtedly had the most outgoing personality of anyone in our class. She radiated happiness at being alive. She spoke to everyone who passed her. She was quite a good student, and was more than willing to help any student who needed additional help. She would not *give* you the answers, but she would assist you in thinking a problem through until you understood it. Thus, she gave you *two* gifts . . . the immediately needed answer *and* the relative information you could later apply to other circumstances. And she was forever smiling! She was the type of girl all mothers would want as a friend for their daughter.

But I missed a wonderful opportunity with this girl, for I never allowed myself to become acquainted with her. I have wondered many times over the years what I sacrificed in refusing to be her friend. She had tried to befriend me on many occasions, but I was always in a rush to retrieve something I had left behind, to hurry into the next class, or fly off for an appointment. She was a really neat person . . . a good and considerate individual, but I simply could not be her friend.

For, you see, she was not one of the "beautiful people."

She suffered from abnormalities. Her speech was slurred and difficult to understand. But I didn't have a severe problem with that . . . for I never gave her much of an opportunity to say *anything* to me!

I did not make ugly or nasty comments to her, and I did not make sneering faces at her.

But I did abuse her.

On many occasions.

I abused her by neglecting and ignoring her. I made her feel rejected by clearly communicating that she did not qualify for "my world." She lacked the necessary exterior appearance, and I simply *could* not (or *would* not) get past that hurdle.

I have wondered about her many times over the years.

Did she ever reach her full potential?

What type of career did she pursue?

Did she ever marry and have a family?

Did she ultimately find a circle of friends?

I never became her friend. And I was the loser.

For had I been willing to learn, she could have taught me many lessons of life . . . lessons in compassion, in determination, in understanding, in courage, in true friendship, and in gallant living in spite of overwhelming odds. But because I did not give her the opportunity to teach me, I had to learn these lessons later in my life, when the going got harder . . . and the price went higher.

We would be wise to remember, "That which is striking and beautiful is not always good, but that which is good is always beautiful."

Christmas Past

We were nearing the end of December . . . another month, another year . . . and Christmas was but a memory of 48 hours before.

Thanksgiving had passed and all minds shifted to "holiday" mode. We noticed that all of society changed before our eyes. There were the usual decorations found on the fronts of homes, lighted sculptures in the yard, and colorful adornments within the stores.

But it was more than that.

People seemed different.

We saw folks smiling more often, speaking to strangers more frequently, and showing more common courtesy. Although shoppers were searching (sometimes frantically) for that perfect gift for their special someone, they seemed to primarily enjoy their task. Everyone appeared to be caught up in the moment. Anticipation was running high. Enthusiasm was everywhere. Being around people was fun . . . except, perhaps, for the occasional Scrooge whose body language shouted, "Bah. Humbug!" But every Christmas has its one or two bad apples. It goes with the territory.

When the holiday was over, I could take my time and leisurely stroll through the stores and watch for any after-Christmas bargains that might come my way. And do you know what I saw?

People.

People with that old familiar un-holiday look about them.

The magic of Christmas was gone!

And in its place? The customary sights and sounds of people

on a mission that exemplified the "I'm looking for something, and you better get out of my way" countenance about them.

The day seemed even sadder when I heard one gentleman remark to his wife (who was also looking for bargains), "Why do you want Christmas stuff? Christmas is over."

As I stood in the aisle contemplating the man's comment, I found myself thinking, "That's sad. But he is right."

To millions of people around the globe, Christmas is a one-day event, the crowning moment of home-baked goodies, colorful wrapping paper, curly ribbon bows, seasonal music, and granted wishes. It is a day for delicious dinners with all the trimmings . . . and chats by the fireplace. It is a day for *peace on earth and good will toward men*.

But what about December 28th, or February 3rd, or June 16th, or August 7th? What about the other 364 days of the year?

Is the spirit of giving, generosity, and kindness to be placed on the shelf and resurrected next December?

We must remember that the best kind of Christmas **giving** is Christmas **living**! ALL YEAR LONG!

Who? Me?

American journalist Diane Sawyer once stated, "There is no substitute for paying attention."

What simple advice!

Yet how profound!

We teach our children to be quiet. To listen. To watch. To *pay attention* to what takes place around them. Yet we, as adults, forget that primary lesson. We live in our hectic world and move at our frantic pace; we are barely conscious of our surroundings.

We hear something important and tell ourselves we must remember it. Yet we promptly forget it.

We see something we wish to recapture in our mind. Yet before we realize what has happened, the details have fallen into oblivion.

We smell an enticing aroma and tell ourselves we shall forever retain its pleasantness. Yet before we turn the calendar page, we think no more of it.

We taste a delectable treat on our taste buds and tell our palate to indelibly make a record of it. Yet before we can find the words to adequately describe it in the days that follow, it has gone out of our head.

I stumbled upon a short piece of poetry recently (author unknown) that offered wise advice on this matter of remembering, forgetting, and paying attention:

Always remember to forget

The things that made you sad.

But never forget to remember

The things that made you glad.

If you were busy being true

To what you knew you ought to do,

You'd be so busy, you'd forget

The blunders of the folks you met.

There is a definite connection between our powers of observation of the world around us . . . and the precious gift of memory. Someone eloquently stated, "Our memories allow us to smell flowers in winter." That is assuming, of course, that we put our memory to its best use by remembering to forget the unpleasant things.

What a wonderful world this would be if we could forget our troubles as easily as we forget our blessings.

So simple.

Yet so profound.

College Friends – Then and Now

Cathie Rizco came onto the college campus totally unaware that Carol Goodman existed. I didn't know she existed, either. But we were soon to meet and strike a friendship that has lasted more than 30 years.

The year was 1965, and Cathie was an incoming freshman. I was beginning my junior year. Perhaps we never would have met if we hadn't been assigned to the same floor of the same dormitory. But we were. And we did.

The minute we spoke to each other, we knew we did not come from the same area of the country. She hailed from New Jersey, and I claimed Ohio as my home state. Cathie had the typical New Jersey accent, referring to that cold drink as *soda*, while I called it *pop*. When we went to the grocery together, she asked for paper *bags*, while I asked for *sacks*. She said she had to wash her *sneakers,* while I washed my *tennis shoes*. But we quickly overcame the "language barrier" and continued to learn one another's vocabulary.

We were attending a small Christian college, where I was one of 1200 Protestant students. Cathie was the only Catholic student. I never brought up the topic of religion with her, for I saw too many other students doing that. I didn't become her friend in an attempt to "convert" her. I became her friend because I *liked* her.

Cathie was of Italian-Polish descent, while I reigned from German and Irish background. Cathie's skin was that golden bronze, and she had the most striking brown hair and eyes that were so brown, they often looked black. I, on the other hand, was fair-skinned, light-haired, and blue-eyed.

She was the cheerleader. I was the book worm. She liked the party life, while I liked the quieter life. We were so very different in so many ways. But beneath all the differences, a friendship was forging that would continue until this day.

There were not a lot of activity options in this small college town, and Cathie and I discovered we did have something in common, after all. We both were quite good at thinking up creative things to do. Neither of us had much money, and neither of us owned a car. But we enjoyed ourselves nonetheless.

I remember one day in particular when we were especially bored. It was final-exam week, and we had reached our saturation point with facts, figures, theories, and books in general. We put our heads together and decided to have an adventure-filled afternoon. We each grabbed a pocketful of the shiniest pennies we could find, along with some nails we found lying around. We then headed for the less prestigious part of town near the railroad tracks.

As we headed for our destination, we threw ourselves completely into an academic discussion of the old adage, "They're from the other side of the tracks." I had heard the expression before but had never thought much about it. But as we watched the tracks appear closer and closer, we decided to discuss the matter at length. What exactly did "from the other side of the tracks" mean? We both stood on the same side of the tracks and said the folks on the opposite side were "from the other side of the tracks."

Then we both stepped to the opposite side, and suddenly realized that the people we had just been standing with were suddenly "from the other side of the tracks." And then we split and each stood on an opposite of the tracks. Now we had a dilemma. Which of us was "from the other side of the tracks"? We thought about the manner in which people are constantly creating dividing lines, even using something as simple as railroad tracks. We wondered why they didn't think of coming together more often, rather than separating themselves. I think Cathie and I are *still* pondering that one!

After we had a good laugh about the academic ramifications of such a deep subject as railroad tracks, we started walking them. Now, you must remember that this was a sleepy little college town, and there was not much to occupy our minds. It appeared that we both were the victims of brain drain and were desperate to do *anything* to get away from the study mode for a while. We walked until we both thought we were "away from things" sufficiently, stopped, and decided to put our pennies and nails to use.

We chose a stretch of track from which we could see far into the distance in either direction. We may have been desperate college kids, but we were not stupid. We were not about to get caught by surprise as a train rounded a nearby bend. With all the ceremony of a visiting dignitary, we placed the pennies and the nails in precisely the desired location. Some were in straight lines, some rode piggy-back on each other, and some were in fanciful designs. I even recall that we had had the presence of mind to take along some scotch tape . . . to hold our items in place on the tracks when they began to rumble under the vibration of the approaching train.

I'm sure you have heard the old expression, "A watched pot never boils." Well, a watched railroad track didn't seem to accommodate a train, either. We waited for what seemed like hours. But finally we heard the whistle that blew the warning . . . the warning that we had best be sufficiently out of the path of the oncoming train . . . and the warning that our **art work** was soon to become permanently entangled. Can you believe that as that train ran over our pennies and nails, we were actually excited to see what the end result would be?

We never did find some of the pennies and nails. But the ones we did locate were a treasure that occupied their proper place of distinction back in our dorm rooms! The other girls would come into our rooms and ask what those *mangled messes* were. With righteous indignation, Cathie and I informed our friends that those *mangled messes* were true pieces of art . . . created by us and the local train tracks, with some help from the train and the engineer, of course.

During another weekend that was rather dull, Cathie and I decided we would go sun-bathing in a nearby pasture. The local farmer was a good-natured old fellow who understood that college girls needed a place for such activity, and he permitted us on his land. We had completed our usual sun worship thing and were heading back to the campus. It was a rather long walk, most of which was through the pasture. We had made this trek many times and could have done it in our sleep. But our routine dream date with the sun was about to turn to an unexpected nightmare.

Our of nowhere came this monstrous-sized stallion who apparently liked the smell of our baby oil . . . or something. Neither Cathie nor I had realized **Big Boy** was loose in the field that day. But as he came thundering toward us, we did not take time to discuss the matter. We headed straight for the fence and what we thought would be safety. Now *I* was the one who was a member of the college gymnastic team, not Cathie. But she suddenly gained the speed and skill of a distance runner and pole-vaulter all rolled into one. She headed toward that fence like a bullet.

To this day, I'm not sure why I lingered a minute longer. Perhaps I thought the old four-legged dude would suddenly change his mind.

He didn't!

Perhaps I thought he would change his direction.

He didn't!

Cathie was safely on the other side of the fence when **Big Boy's** teeth sunk into my shoulder.

Now I had been bitten by cats before. And I had been bitten by dogs before. And I had been bitten by rabbits before.

But I had *never* been bitten by a HORSE before!

He sunk his teeth into me and held on for dear life. It was obvious that he had no plans to let go any time in the near future. I was scared. I was in pain. And I was mad . . . mad at that obnoxious horse for biting me, mad at myself for getting caught in that predicament, and made at Cathie because **she was safely over the fence!**

I tried pulling away from that huge animal, but it was no use. He had attacked from behind, so I couldn't even turn around to strike him. Finally, I remembered the bottle of baby oil in my right hand. I took that bottle, reached across my left shoulder, and began pounding that horse's nose for all I was worth! I didn't care if the bottle was plastic or glass. I didn't care if it broke. I didn't care if it spilled all over me. I just wanted that awful horse to let go of me! And all the while, I was screaming, "C-A-T-H-I-E! H-E-L-P!" over and over.

We have laughed about this incident many times over the years, and Cathie admits to having a real struggle within herself. She was safety out of reach of the horse's teeth. But her friend was in trouble. She climbed back into the "wild horse arena," and both of us somehow managed to break me free from that wretched animal. As we sprang over the fence, I'm not sure which were racing faster . . . our *feet* or our *hearts.*

We arrived back on campus and began surveying the damage to my body. It didn't take a medically-inclined person to realize that I had one badly bitten and bruised shoulder. And Cathie and I were smart enough to know that I needed a tetanus shot. Talk about adding insult to injury! I have never minded needles, but tetanus shots are not the most pleasant thing in the world. But I did my duty and visited the nearby doctor's office.

I decided it would be in my best interest not to tell my parents about the horse-biting incident. I knew that my mother, being a nurse, would worry about it until she saw me at spring break. So I said nothing during the last few letters and phone calls. Once home for the week of spring, I decided my mother would probably be upset that I hadn't told her about the horse bite, so I decided never to say anything.

The next afternoon as I was soaking in my own personal bathtub after a week of final exams, my mother walked in unexpectedly. She had not realized I was there, but it took her only about 3 seconds to see the ugly red, black, blue, yellow, and green shoulder that protruded from the bubbles.

In absolute shock she asked, "What happened to you??!!"

Never in my wildest dreams did I think she would ever know. Never did I think I would be called upon for an explanation. My mind went blank. I can remember myself feebly saying, "I was bitten."

"By WHAT!"

"A horse."

"A **horse**! WHY didn't you say something? Did you get a tetanus shot? WHEN did this happen? HOW did it happen? Has a doctor looked at it recently? Are you all right?"

Good grief! Was this woman a reporter, or what?

Later, after my own children were born, I realized she was simply being a mother. A mother who had been shocked. A mother who cared. A mother who loved me.

Cathie and I met back at school the following quarter and

continued our friendship, our pranks, our good times, our serious conversations, and all the other things that go into a lasting relationship.

I graduated, married, and lived in Ohio for several years before moving to Kentucky. Cathie graduated, married, and lived in New Jersey and Missouri before moving to Texas. I suffered the death of a child. Cathie suffered the death of a marriage. Cathie's older child is a daughter, as is mine. Her younger child is a son, as is mine. I have raised my children with the help of a supportive husband. Cathie has raised her children with the struggles of being a single mother. Cathie lost both of her parents by age 46. I lost both my parents by age 46. Cathie and I have continued to share our love of the outdoors, of children, and of cooking.

So many differences. So many similarities. How often our paths have separated. How often they have crossed. The miles have taken us apart, but the phone calls and letters have kept us together.

Yet, in spite of it all, we have remained friends . . . then and now! True friendship can endure similarities, differences, distances, traumas, and routines. We *can* enjoy the blessings of life-long friendships.

Is there someone in your life that means a great deal to you . . . someone you do not often see or speak with or write to? Is it someone you have suddenly felt the urge to contact and make connection with again?

Do it! Do it today! Why wait until tomorrow? Those things that we put off until tomorrow have a way of never getting accomplished. Isn't your connection with this person worth the effort it will cost you to contact him or her?

Humble Pie

Humility is perhaps the only human characteristic that, once we realize we have it, we have lost it. And exactly what *is* humility? Most Americans over the age of eight know what it is, but it is one of those words that is rather difficult to define. Humility is *not* viewing oneself as inferior or worthless or not contributing to society.

Humility is also not humiliation. But, conversely, we must learn that if we do not learn humility within ourselves, we *will* learn humiliation at the hands of others.

Humility is, quite simply, being aware of one's defects or shortcomings. Or, as Charles Spurgeon (the great American preacher) stated, it is "making a right estimate of oneself." And lest we think that such awareness is a negative albatross around our necks, we must remind ourselves that awareness of any true state of ourselves brings great insight and strength and resolve. John Ruskin, said by some to be one of the most influential English critics of the 1800s, went so far as to state, "The first test of a truly great man is his humility."

Most of us, at one point or another, have been reminded that it is our time for a serving of humble pie. But perhaps we are not aware of the origin of such food and think that it is merely an expression of embarrassment. But historically, humble pie was actually made from the inner parts of a deer and was given to the servants after a hunt.

A diplomat once called on President Abraham Lincoln and was quite astonished to find him blacking his own shoes. When the diplomat expressed surprise that the Commander-in-Chief of the United States of America would be found in such a common task, Lincoln looked equally surprised and asked, "Whose shoes do you black?" A simple question from a humble man whose beginnings taught him all individuals, regardless of their stance in life, have common responsibilities.

And yet humility, with all of its implications, becomes relative in a very real sense. As Benjamin Franklin once observed, "To be humble with superiors is duty. To be humble with equals is courtesy. But to be humble with inferiors is nobleness." Humility is most gracious when it is bestowed upon the least deserving.

Humility is not denying one's talents or abilities, but it is the ability to see those blessings in their true perspective. And that perspective is also relative. Someone once observed that a mountain shames a molehill until both are humbled by the stars.

So let us all, by reason of our newfound thoughts on the matter, realize that our efforts and contributions to the world around us need not be in competition with those around us. Rather, we should **compliment (praise)** and **complement (complete)** one another.

In other words, let us expend our energy expressing courtesy, respect, admiration, and praise to our fellow humans while we simultaneously do all we can to bring completion to the tasks around us.

"Why?" or "What?"

We suddenly find ourselves in the midst of a traumatic situation, and we beggingly ask, "Why? Why me?" It is a natural response as we thinking humans continually search for answers. At times it seems we are incapable of absorbing the situation unless we can somehow discover the reason behind it.

Perhaps our trauma is watching helplessly while a loved one succumbs to the ravages of a terminal illness. Or a person is taken from us suddenly by accidental death. Our grief is multiplied if that loss is brought about by the carelessness or intentional disrespect for life by others. But in any situation, this heartache is intensified if that loved one is a child, for the death of a child seems to make our entire world slam violently into reverse. We feel all the laws of nature and order have been discarded when older members of a family lay a younger loved one to rest.

Perhaps our trauma is being the victim of a senseless crime, whereby our sense of decency and security is violated. It is at this point in time we realize that, in spite of our best efforts, we can control the environment around us only to a certain point.

Perhaps our trauma is the loss of our home through a natural disaster. Not only is the housing structure splintered after the onslaught of a tornado or earthquake or hurricane, but also our dreams and hopes for the future as well. We stand in shock and confusion as we attempt to devise a plan for putting our lives back together again. Where do we begin to pick up the pieces of bricks and boards, of curtains and furniture, of pictures and china? But more importantly, where do we begin to pick up the pieces of our emotions?

Perhaps our trauma is the loss of valued personal items through burglary. We consider the monetary value of such loss, but many times that loss goes much deeper as we realize we no longer possess that special item given to us by someone very special. It was, perhaps, our link to the past; perhaps it was a link to a present relationship. Or perhaps it was an item that was to play a vital role in our future. But whatever the time frame represented, that special possession is no longer ours. And we regret it deeply.

Perhaps our trauma is a dream gone astray resulting from a poor decision we made. Perhaps it is the consequence of a choice made in the heat of anger. Perhaps it is a once-friendly relationship that has been destroyed by rumor, gossip, and misunderstanding.

But whatever the trauma, we must realize we have a choice in how we respond. We need not stand by pathetically asking ourselves, "Why?"

Rather, we have the opportunity to ask ourselves, "What?"

What can we take from this heartache and apply to other circumstances in life?

What learning experience can we gain from this trauma?

What can we take from this experience to help others who pass through similar heartache?

How can we take our hurt and sorrow . . . and somehow make a better world in which to live because we walked through that dark period in our lives?

If we pass through the shadows of heartache, but gain value from it, it is nonetheless sorrowful. But if we remain in those shadows of heartache, demanding answers that we may never receive in this life, this experience is pitifully tragic.

The decision is ours.

And we will live with the consequences of that decision.

The Stolen Popsicle

I was just a kid when it happened. I played with the neighbor girl named Sherry. I can't recall her last name, but *Sherry* will suffice. My parents were not all that keen on me playing with her, for she came from a home where her family taught lower moral values than did my family. But since there were not any other kids in the neighborhood at the time, my folks realized my choices were few and far between. So they would occasionally permit me to spend time with Sherry.

It was a hot summer day, and Sherry appeared at my back door with a popsicle in her hand, wanting to know if I could come out and play. My mother agreed, so Sherry and I thought we would have the afternoon to ourselves. Wrong!

Every time Sherry licked that popsicle, it looked more and more tempting to me. Finally she said, "Why don't you go next door to the grocery store and get yourself a popsicle?"

It sounded like a good idea, but I had to admit that I didn't have any money. I had spent all my allowance, and my mother was not all that great at advancing me money. I realize now she was attempting to teach me good money management, but at that point in history, I assumed it was because she simply didn't want me to have the finer things in life.

When Sherry realized my predicament, she offered a workable solution. She looked at me with those deeply set eyes of hers and shook her head in disbelief that I had not thought of the same solution.

"Well, just go in the store and take one," she said. "The owner will never miss one popsicle."

She was right. He wouldn't miss one popsicle.

I was wrong.

I followed her advice.

I do not remember my following thoughts, but I *do* know I realized what I was about to do was wrong. I had been taught not to steal. If I didn't pay for it, or someone didn't give it to me, it was not mine. Plain and simple. But somehow all that training went out the window as I followed Sherry into the grocery.

I truly do not remember actually stealing the popsicle, but I certainly remember what followed shortly thereafter.

I was still enjoying my good frozen treat on that hot summer day when my mother appeared on the scene. Knowing I did not have any allowance left, she said, "Where did you get that popsicle?"

"In the store?"

She didn't respond immediately, and I felt a sudden sense of relief. I *knew* she wasn't going to pursue the matter.

Wrong again!

I spent a lot of my childhood being wrong where my mother was concerned. Perhaps you had the same experience.

It was very difficult to ruffle my mother's feathers, so in her usual calm manner, she continued, "But you don't have any allowance money left."

Uh, oh. "Hot seat" time!

I was smart enough to know that I didn't know what to say. So I kept silent, hoping my mother would go away.

I should have known better. My mother **never** just "went away."

"So how did you buy the popsicle?"

That "hot seat" was getting hotter . . . quickly!

I was smart enough to realize I had been busted, so I simply said, "I took it."

"No. You mean you stole it." And did she ever emphasize that word *stole!* I felt as if a knife had been plunged into me. Now my mother was a registered surgical nurse, so perhaps that is why she always cut to the meat of the matter . . . quickly and efficiently. She had had a lot of practice in the operating room. And right now, I was the patient on the table. And that table was becoming extremely uncomfortable.

I remember my pathetic attempt at trying to justify my actions and explaining that it wasn't really stealing. Externally, my mother was still unruffled and asked that awful final question, "Then what is it . . . really?"

I was completely disarmed. I had no further answers, and I knew it.

Mama didn't even wait for an answer. She took me by the arm . . . not all that gently, either . . . and marched me into the grocery store. By this time, the popsicle was nearly gone, but that made no difference to my mother. She didn't care whether the popsicle was outside or inside my body. The point was . . . I had stolen something, and I was about to face the consequences.

She marched me straight to the owner and said to me, "Don't you have something to tell Mr. Tice?"

What in the world was this woman doing to me? Didn't she love me at all? Didn't she care I was feeling such humiliation that I would have welcomed the floor opening up and swallowing me? Didn't she have any concern over the effect this trauma would have on my psyche? Didn't she have any compassion for this poor little kid who had been talked into doing something wrong by her friend? After all, I hadn't suggested the idea. Sherry had.

I was looking at myself in terms of that particular day. My mother was looking at me in terms of the kind of person I would become later in life.

So there we stood . . . Mr. Tice, my mother, and me.

Mr. Tice looked bewildered. My mother looked determined. And I am sure I looked totally downtrodden. I had never been so embarrassed in my entire life. What was this woman trying to do to me?

I mumbled and stumbled around, trying to get the words out. But those words had grabbed my vocal chords, and I couldn't seem to say anything.

Perhaps if my mother could see me suffering enough, she would show a little compassion and tell Mr. Tice herself. I realize now that I must have been one dumb kid! My mother had no such intentions! Any explanation that was given would come from my mouth, and mine alone!

Suddenly Mr. Tice realized what had happened, and I was never so grateful to hear someone say, "That's all right. It was just one popsicle." I was so grateful for his compassion that I could have kissed him. At least *one* person in my midst wanted to spare me further humiliation.

But my sense of relief did not last long. I heard my mother, that woman who was supposed to love me and protect me, say, "No, sir, it is **not** all right. She stole something, and she is going to admit it and apologize, even if it takes all day."

I knew she meant every word she said, and that if I did not hurry up and apologize, I would literally be standing there all day. So I finally succeeded in getting the words out. I thought the matter was over. But I had forgotten something. I still owed Mr. Tice a nickel for the popsicle. (Yes, popsicles cost only a nickel back in those days.)

The nightmare scenario ended with my mother telling Mr. Tice that I would be back to pay him his nickel as soon as I had earned it.

Now, this was early afternoon, and I felt certain that I would be returning to Mr. Tice within a short time. After all, how much work would I have to do to earn a nickel? But I had forgotten who I was dealing with. My mother was no push-over, and she was teaching her a daughter a lesson that would remain with her the rest of her life.

I remember seeing the look on my mother's face. It was not one of enjoyment. It was not one of satisfaction. But rather it was a look of hurt and disappointment. I knew that, in spite of all my mother was putting me through, she loved me, and she wanted me to develop into the very best person I could become. She also knew I would never do that if I did not learn at a young age that improper actions come with a high price tag!

My mother hated what I *had done*. But I knew with every fiber of my being that she did not hate *me!*

My mother was not a slave driver, and she did not approve of child labor. But be assured and please believe me when I tell you that I worked the remainder of that entire day . . . doing every chore imaginable to earn that nickel. It was not the nickel I would remember paying back. It was the labor and the giving of myself that I would remember. And my mom was smart enough to know that; so she made sure I invested *plenty* of my time and myself so I could remember it well.

The next day, I went to Mr. Tice and properly paid for the popsicle. But I paid a higher price than he would ever know. And in the process, I learned more than I had paid.

First a Popsicle, Then Clothing

Any girl with the sense that God gave a wild goose would certainly have learned her lesson about stealing, wouldn't she? With all the trauma I had experienced during the popsicle incident, one would certainly think so. But I must have been suffering from a terminal case of DUMB, for I didn't seem to remember what I had previously learned.

I was in my early teens, and my family was having great financial difficulty. There were several articles of clothing I needed that the family budget simply could not accommodate. One of those items was a half slip that was the proper length. I continued to manage on what I had, but I desperately wanted that particular type of slip.

I was spending the afternoon at a neighborhood friend's house (**not** Sherry's house) and was shocked to realize this girl had not one, but several, half slips. She certainly didn't need them all. After all, she could wear only one at a time.

To this day, I cannot believe what I did next.

When my friend left the room, I stuffed one of those slips into my clothing and quickly made an excuse to go home. Needless to say, I had to stash that slip where it would be safe . . . so I could enjoy wearing it later.

The first truth I discovered was that I could not enjoy wearing something that did not rightfully belong to me. The second truth I discovered was that time did not always erase guilt. For every time I wore that slip, I continued to think about what I had done. And there was not much pleasure in that.

The friend and I continued to be friends (although I always felt uncomfortable in her presence) through high school and college.

The years passed. I had married and become a professional

135

working woman. But Father Time had not permitted me to forget about that stolen slip. Each time I reached a point in my life where I was feeling pretty good about myself and the contribution I was making to young lives in the classroom by my example, I would remember that slip. It was like an albatross around my neck I could not destroy.

Finally, I admitted there was no solution to my problem except the *right* solution. I had been playing mind games with myself, and I kept losing the game.

I was tired of losing, and I was ready to make things right. I kept wondering what Mr. Tice would think if he could see the mess I was in . . . again!

A little more than 10 years had passed since I stole the slip. I had actually thrown the thing away not long after I stole it, hoping its destination in the city dump would alleviate my guilt. But it hadn't, and it was time for action.

One day after I received my paycheck, I went to the nicest clothing store in town and bought my friend a new half slip. Buying it was the easy part. The hard part was giving it to her, along with an explanation of what had transpired ten years before and the ensuing guilt I hard carried for a decade.

I went to her and gave her the slip, along with the explanation, "I know you can't imagine why I am giving you this item, but I stole one from you ten years ago. I have bought a replacement and have left the price tag on it so that you may return it if you want another article of clothing."

She looked at me as if speechless but finally stammered, "You don't have to do this. It was so long ago, just forget it."

She didn't seem to realize that I *had* tried to forget it.

For ten years I had tried forgetting it, but to no avail.

I was doing the only thing possible to make matters right.

We must never forget that there are no painless short-cuts in making things right with our fellow humans. But we must make things right nonetheless. And if, by chance, we do not learn our lesson the first time around, we must not fail ourselves and those around us by not continuing to do our best at making things right with our fellow humans.

Deadly Discontent

There once was a man and his wife who had purchased their ideal house in the suburbs. It was the perfect home with a grand view, more than adequate amounts of sunlight and space, the desired floor plan, and a strong, substantial neighborhood.

But the fault-finding began a few years later as the couple became dissatisfied with their home . . . generally trivial objections the husband and wife had permitted to take on more-than-usual importance in their lives. Realizing their unhappiness was growing each day, the couple decided to put their house up for sale and began searching for their dream house once again.

In the daily paper, the couple saw an advertisement that perfectly described the house for which they were searching. Upon calling the listing agent, they were shocked to discover that the home they wanted to visit was their very own.

A similar tale is told of a certain man who lived in Baghdad and dreamed one night that there was a certain street in Cairo where he would find a precious treasure.

The man began his journey into Egypt and, along the way, met a man who was traveling from Cairo to Baghdad. This man also had had a dream in which he was told to search for a treasure in a particular house in Baghdad.

As the days progressed, each man realized he had been sent to the other's house to find a treasure that needed merely to be searched for by the owner.

As we look upon the foolishness of such stories, must we not admit to ourselves that we, too, have permitted seeds of discontent to yield a garden of disgruntlement within our own lives?

Do we not sometimes find ourselves caught up in the disappointment of a particular situation that we felt would bring us our longed-for satisfaction and delight?

What happens when we begin our journey to locate our sought-after dreams of fulfillment, only to discover later that they do not provide us with our visions of gratification?

John D. Rockefeller (one of the most famous names in American business, finance, and philanthropy) was once the world's richest individual. It is estimated that he gave away approximately $550 million in his lifetime. During a media interview, Rockefeller was asked, "How much money does it take to make a man happy?"

His insightful answer gave many clues into human nature and overwhelming greed when he responded, "Just a little bit more!" Most of us would have to agree with Rockefeller as we stop to realize that we are rarely contented. There is always something else we would like to possess.

What does this say about our internal value system?

What does this indicate about our priorities?

A tourist in Mexico stopped one day to watch the village women as they did their laundry in a hot spring and cold spring that were situated side by side. The foreigner was taken aback by the convenience of nature's blessing, and as he continued observing the women wash their clothing in the hot spring and rinse them in the cold spring, he remarked, "Nature sure is generous."

"Yes," replied one of the Mexican women, "but some of these people complain that Nature doesn't provide free soap."

Such ingratitude!

Such selfishness!

Yet have we never looked at our multitude of blessings and heard ourselves lament, "If only I had [whatever], I would be happy"? Are we not like the Mexican women who complained of no soap?

A long-ago learned piece of poetry keeps running through my mind that chastised us by saying "I complained of having no shoes until I met a man who had no feet."

As long as we place our importance on external things rather than what is inside us, we will never find true contentment. We would be wise to always remember Ben Franklin's advice: "Contentment makes poor men rich, while discontentment makes rich men poor."

Perhaps the mark of truly contented individuals are those who can enjoy the scenery along the detour.

The story is told of two children who were living happily in their father's house. But they would often gaze upon another house standing atop a distant hill. As the evening sun would set each night, the window panes of the hilltop house would glisten with the sparkles of millions of rubies, sapphires, emeralds, and diamonds. It was a breath-taking sight, indeed!

After watching the evening spectacle for many weeks, the children set off to visit the distant house, knowing within their hearts that they would see a picture of indescribable beauty from within the home.

After trudging through running creeks, stumbling over moss-covered rocks, and falling into rambling thorn bushes, their dreams were shattered as they found the house empty and barren. Years of collected dust covered both the inside and the outside of the hilltop house. As the weary children continued to look at the desolate and bleak house, they turned to begin their trek home. But they fell silent as they beheld the glorious splendor of the sun's rays upon their own home.

And in that moment of time, the children learned a valuable lesson . . . it is not the *reflected* light, but the *inner* light, that shines in a home and makes it worthy of the joy and hope and refuge it offers.

Let us learn the same lesson!

United We Stand, Divided We Fall

During World War II, an army officer spoke to his men as they stood in formation. He explained that volunteers were needed immediately for a dangerous mission. The captain was brutally frank concerning the hazardous duty involved, the jeopardy in which the men would find themselves, and the slim chances of all of them returning safety home. At the conclusion of his detailed explanation, the captain asked any volunteers to take three steps forward.

At precisely that moment, a courier arrived with an urgent message from the captain's superior. He turned to read the message and quickly compiled a written response.

As the officer turned again toward his men, he felt a sense of alarm and disappointment as he saw the unbroken line. He began chastising them for their cowardice, their unwillingness to serve their country in a time of desperate need, and their apparent primary concern for their own selfish well-being.

Suddenly one of the enlisted men spoke up and said, "But, sir, as you were reading the message, we all moved forward three paces. Each of us wants to volunteer."

As persons who have served in the armed forces tell us, troops are ordered to break stride as they approach a bridge. For it is a well-established fact that the strength and precision of many feet stepping in perfect unison will weaken and possibly collapse such a structure.

Yet we forget such basic rules of conduct in our daily living. We struggle for our personal individuality to reign supreme. We insist that our own desires be initially recognized. We argue that our particular priorities be given first consideration. And in the midst of these self-focused desires, we often break away from the team in pursuit of our own goals. When we should be marching forward in unison, we break stride to follow our own "yellow brick road."

A Chinese emperor was ruling his dynasty, and being quite elderly, he was concerned that he find the proper heir to follow him . . . an heir that would show courage, strength, and wisdom. He called each of his eight sons together, instructing them to bring one arrow each. As the emperor and his offspring gathered, the old man tied the eight arrows together with twine. He then instructed each son to attempt to break the arrows.

The first son tried to break the bundle with all his strength, but he failed. The second son attempted. He also failed. The third son, too, failed.

The fourth son, determined to be the victor, mustered every ounce of strength he could call upon in his attempt to break the bundle. And he showed great remorse when his efforts proved futile.

The fifth son, wise beyond his years, untied the twine, separated the bundle, and broke each arrow individually with minimal effort.

The emperor immediately chose the fifth son as his successor to the throne, for the old man knew within his heart that this young man had the wisdom to understand human nature and the insight to conquer his enemies.

The fifth son, although not the eldest nor the strongest, knew: "United, we stand. Divided, we fall."

Balanced Memories

There is the story of an ancient Greek woman who appeared at the River Styx to be carried to the waiting world of departed spirits. As the woman was making her final preparation for the journey, her escort told her that she could drink from the waters of Lethe if she wanted to forget all of her earthly existence. She was thrilled at such an opportunity and exclaimed, "Yes, then I shall forget all my pain and suffering."

"But you will also forget your joys and happiness," reminded her escort.

"I shall forget all the times I have been hated by others," voiced the old woman.

"Yes, but you will also forget how you have been loved."

" I shall forget my failures," observed the old woman.

"Yes, and also your victories and triumphs."

The old woman pondered her escort's words. Her future would be determined by her present choice of past experiences. She continued to reflect upon her decision until she knew within herself what she must do.

She would not drink of the magic waters.

The price was simply too high.

Disposing of life's painful memories would not be worth losing the memories of joy and happiness.

And we, today, must also understand the significance of our remembrances. Someone once wisely stated, "It is never too late to have a happy childhood." Our hearts and minds are capable of recapturing those precious times of the past that brought delight to our souls and light to our paths. We can relive the enchanting days of the past that brought waves of well-being into our very essence.

We cannot always control what life delivers to us, but we *can* control the surrounding thoughts that shape our days. It is within our power to tightly hold the gladness we have been privileged to share. And it is also within our power to discard the anguish and the affliction.

The choice is ours.

And we, alone, must make that choice.

We must always remember that one of the best uses of our memory is to remember to forget the unpleasant things. Or to look at the unpleasant thing in perspective so we know what we would do differently the next time.

Left-Over Pieces

There once was a man who had been contracted to build a great cathedral. But as he progressed in his work each day, a young apprentice continued to pester him. The young man wanted to design the glass for just one window of the magnificent church. Each day, the young apprentice asked the master to allow him to help. Each day, the old master declined, knowing that the young man had not yet acquired the skills necessary to complete such a task.

After many days, the old master realized the young man's determination. The old master also realized that if he continued refusing the young man's requests, he might be discouraging the apprentice from future ambitions. But neither did the old master want to risk wasting valuable materials.

Finally the old master agreed to allow the young man to attempt the design of one small window. But there was one stipulation. The young apprentice would have to supply the materials himself.

Unfaltering in his determination and courage, the young man gathered up all the left-over pieces of glass that the other workmen had discarded. He began to quietly and persistently arrange his bits and pieces until he completed a window of rare beauty and design.

When the cathedral was opened to the public, crowds stood in silent wonder and reverence of the one small window that had been designed by the apprentice. The beauty was breathtaking as each piece of glass transformed the filtered sunlight into a glorious symphony of unified precision.

At difficult times in our lives, do we find ourselves sulking and bemoaning the fact that life seems to have handed us simply the left-over pieces? Do we stew in our dissatisfaction and frustration, thinking of the accomplishments we could achieve if only life had given us a better share of the "good things"? Do we find ourselves becoming resentful and jealous of others as they seem to be continuously blessed with good fortune?

At such times, we should remember the young apprentice. He did not receive his precious glass that he so desired. Yet in spite of being deprived of his desire, he gathered what he could and, with his best efforts, constructed something of even greater beauty than others anticipated. And its beauty was compounded by the fact that he had created it from the left-over pieces.

Do you have left-over pieces of your life lying around? Perhaps we all do, in one form or another. And if so, it is our choice as to whether we will allow them to remain useless or whether we will make something of value or beauty from them.

We are free to make that ultimate decision; but we must do so with the knowledge that we will live with the consequences of our decision. Are we willing to put forth the determination and effort to create our own life's "stained glass window"?

Passing People

While sitting in the lobby of a large hotel, I found myself studying the hotel's physical features. I wondered how it was humanly possible to keep that huge crystal chandelier so sparkling and brilliant. I wondered whose responsibility it was and when it was cleaned. I've been in hotel lobbies early in the morning, in the afternoon, and late at night. And I have *never* seen anyone cleaning a chandelier.

I watched the large ceiling fans slowly turning as they kept the air circulating so the patrons could enjoy a fresher environment. I began to sense the relaxation that the slowly spinning wooden blades were creating in me. I realized the almost-hypnotizing effect they were having on my consciousness.

I looked intently at the beautifully carved open staircase that led to the upper floors, and I found myself wondering how many trees had been sacrificed for the man-made piece of art. The wood was dark and rich, and it complimented the crystal chandelier magnificently. Such a contrast! The crystal appeared so delicate and soft, while the staircase commanded such strength and determination.

And then I realized how many pieces of luggage on wheels I was seeing. Hardly anyone was *carrying* their baggage; they were *pulling* it. I wondered how heartily the folks of old would laugh if they had been told back then that the time would come when we pulled our luggage?

The sliding doors were opening and closing constantly as people hurriedly entered and exited the lobby. Why was everyone in such a hurry? Were their matters of business truly that urgent, or has hurrying become an automatic way of life for us Americans? Do we hustle and bustle through life without even being aware of our haste? Do we abruptly rush through life, completely unaware of the smaller blessings we are missing? Or perhaps even the larger blessings?

Since it was the Christmas season, I was especially appreciating the beauty of the elaborately decorated Christmas tree laden with large gold, silver, and red ornaments. Their luster was enhanced by the clear mini-lights and red velvet bows that were spaced appropriately. The graceful white doves all appeared to have their attention directed toward the elegant white angel atop the tree. Several large, attractively wrapped packages lay beneath the tree, adding additional festive color and decor.

But sitting in that gateway of activity, absorbing my surroundings, I was suddenly aware of the variety of people passing through that lobby and, in a sense, passing through my life. They were all so much alike, yet so completely different. There were the two young gentlemen, very smartly dressed, walking briskly in step with one another, chatting as quickly as they strode. Their dashing appearance and spirit emulated energy, vitality, excitement, and animation.

A middle-aged woman came hurrying into the lobby, obviously distressed. She looked frustrated and fearful as she frantically asked the porter to *p-l-e-a-s-e* find her luggage. Was there a particular item in her luggage that she could not face tomorrow without?

Did those pieces of luggage contain family jewels that represented her past ancestry and future financial security? Perhaps a *love* memento from her special someone?

Perhaps her cosmetics without which she could not face the general public?

Or perhaps she was concerned over the possible loss of her wardrobe, without which she simply could not be socially acceptable.

Fortunately, the lady and her luggage were reunited, and the look of relief washed over her face like the waves of the ocean wash over the beach.

Gone was the worry.

Gone was the tension.

Gone was the fear.

Presently, there was a smile of relaxation on her face.

In just a few moments, two young women who appeared to be in their late 20s came through those busy sliding doors. They were pulling the customary luggage on wheels, but one of them was also carrying two items that one does not usually see in a large luxury hotel lobby. The younger of the two women was carrying a large fluffy pillow and an iron . . . not a small travel-sized iron, but a large stay-at-home-sized iron. Now I can certainly understand the necessity of having both these items, but it merely surprised me to see them. Somehow these two particular objects seemed strangely out of place in this particular setting.

An older gentleman trudged through the lobby, wiping his nose with his large white handkerchief and looking quite ill. He had that particular stoop of individuals who are continuing their daily routine in spite of sickness. I admired his determination, but I was concerned about the millions of germs he might be spreading to those of us who had managed to stay healthy in spite of the terrible, fluctuating climate. Perhaps the old man was merely suffering an intense allergy attack and was of no contagion to anyone, but people cut him a wide path as they passed by. I wonder, is he feeling any better now?

A teenager suddenly appeared and seemed as though he were looking for someone. He had that *I'm-looking-around-but-cannot-locate-the-person-I-am-trying-to-find* countenance to him. He stayed off to himself in the corner of the lobby so that he could oversee all those individuals coming and going, but suddenly his eye caught something. He continued gazing, and one could read his thoughts from the expression on his face. He walked toward the Christmas tree and, ever so subtly, reached down and quickly touched two of the packages under the tree.

Yes, they were empty.

Back to his corner he went to continue his vigil.

In the midst of such varied human traffic, I also took stock of the multitude of businessmen . . . all similarly attired in their dark, two piece suits, dark shoes, light shirts, and well-ordered ties. They nearly reminded me of clones in their striking executive similarity yet, simultaneously, they bore little resemblance to one another. They appeared in all sizes, shapes, and colors.

Some of them carried the look of an automated mentality as they strode through their customary daily routine. Others appeared to be absorbing all the details of their surroundings.

Some of the businessmen walked and talked with the energy of finely-tuned athletes. Others kept a slower pace as they filed past, seeming to express fatigue and weariness. Perhaps they were experiencing the stress and strain of today's business world. We have many colloquial expressions for such wearied appearance that would seem to adequately describe all of us at various points in our life: *bushed, dead-tired, ready to drop, dog-weary, tuckered out, bedraggled,* and *weary-winged* are but a few.

Some of them appeared to have an intense eagerness to drink in the challenges that awaited them, while others spread the message with their body language that they were quite ready to pack it up and head for home.

Some of them radiated business-world youthfulness. Others carried the scars of the business-world veteran. None of them appeared to empathize with the other. Perhaps there was the ever-present reality of identifying more closely with one's peers. Could the older businessmen recall their more youthful energy? Could the younger fellows understand the weariness of their senior colleagues?

Perhaps.

Perhaps not.

The gentleman for whom I was waiting arrived, and we conducted our meeting. He returned to his hotel room to prepare for his evening meal and activities. I returned home to my waiting business calls and my family.

Yet I continued thinking of the individuals whose lives crossed my path but for the briefest of time.

Did the lady with the misplaced luggage come to the realization that she held the most valuable of her possessions within herself . . . those of life and health?

Did the young lady with the pillow and iron enjoy a restful night's sleep and arrive at her next day's responsibilities with neatly pressed clothing?

Did the sickly-looking older gentleman sufficiently recover to pursue his daily obligations? Or did he find it necessary to run up the white flag of surrender and get appropriate bed rest?

Did the teenager finally locate the person for whom he was looking? And did he wonder within himself what he would have done if the packages under the tree had *not* been empty?

And what of the businessmen? Did any of them, at some point in their journey, become conscious of the others? Did they take notice of their similarities *and* their differences?

Or were they too intensely involved in their corporate trans-
actions to appreciate their greatest asset . . . other individuals
around them.

Sleeping Well When the Wind Blows

A sturdy young man asked a farmer for a position as a farm hand, and although the strapping young man exhibited energy and strength, he appeared to be lacking a sense of security and confidence.

"What can you do?" asked the farmer.

"Anything that needs to be done, sir. I can sleep well when the wind blows."

The farmer did not understand what the young man meant by "I sleep well when the wind blows," but he decided to let the matter pass for the time being. Because of the young man's sincerity in wanting work, the farmer hired him.

A few weeks later, a terrible storm awakened the farmer. He rushed to the young man's sleeping quarters and tried unsuccessfully to awaken him. When the farmer could not arouse the young man, he anxiously went to check on things for himself, to ensure that his animals and possessions would survive the weather onslaught.

To the old farmer's amazement, he found that the barn had been locked, the chicken coop had been properly secured, and a wagon load of hay securely covered with a tarpaulin. As he searched his property for other matters that might need attention in order to withstand the storm, the farmer was pleased to discover that nothing had been left to chance.

Then he understood what the young man meant when he said, "I can sleep well when the wind blows."

The young farm hand, though young in body . . . yet wise beyond his years . . . realized that before beginning a project, we must prepare carefully.

And, thus, we must always bear in mind that the prepared man more frequently succeeds, while the unprepared man fails.

Yet how many times we begin an endeavor, realizing we are not fully prepared, but believing that, somehow, circumstances will merely "work out" as they ought! Without preparation, we cannot have a sense of direction; without a sense of direction, we will not have a goal; and without a goal, we will not know when we have that which for we strived at the beginning of our journey.

We frequently joke about "building our plane as we are flying it." And in some instances, that is necessary. But does it happen more frequently than it should? Do we leave things to chance that we should have prepared for? Do we increase the stress and frustration for ourselves by not allowing time for adequate forethought? Do we increase our chance of failure by not allowing consideration for the possible obstacles that we may encounter?

Do we stop to consider that the greatest percentage of victories depends upon preparation?

Sarah Wood Bowersock, (1830-1931), Carol's Maternal Great-Great Grandmother
(photo of family portrait)

. . . about

PIONEER WOMEN

Part I - Introduction

When we hear the term "pioneer women," we instinctively think of the ladies of the West, traveling across the plains in their long skirts and prairie bonnets, enduring the hardships of making the journey in a rough-riding covered wagon. We envision babies born along the way, loved ones dying and being laid to rest in strange and sometimes frightening unfamiliar soil. We attempt to imagine the constant fear of encountering dried-up watering holes, poisonous snakes, and devastating dust storms or unexpected blizzards.

We ponder the opposition these pioneers faced from Mother Nature, the animal world, warring Indian tribes, and the most basic element of time. We try to imagine the frustration of broken wagon wheels, dwindling ammunition supplies, and lack of privacy. We recall the stories of sickness and disease and deprivation and starvation. We wonder if we have the personal reserves within ourselves to make such a daring trek into the unknown.

But there is another group of American pioneer women whose journey into the unknown has been equally frightening . . . whose experiences have been equally difficult to bear . . . whose lives would be forever changed by their endeavors. These women pioneers faced the same anxieties and loneliness and questions their "westward ho" sisters faced. They, too, sometimes faced deprivation and ostracism from their fellow humans. They are the women who first blazed the trails into new endeavors of accomplishment and recognition.

These courageous women faced a seemingly never-ending list of stumbling blocks, barriers, and set-backs as they pursued their dreams and aspirations. Yet they continued on in the face of their own fears and self-doubts. They persevered during the times of their own self-doubt while enduring the loneliness and insult and ridicule placed upon them by others. They were oftentimes viewed as violators of the law . . . the laws of the land and the laws of God. For, after all, women were not "supposed to" be involved in certain areas of endeavor and accomplishment.

These pioneers were told they did not have the right to vote, to hold positions of responsibility and respect, to be doctors and lawyers and engineers and astronauts. They were frowned upon and labeled as "rebels" when they desired to enter the political arena or play a significant part in the business world. Yet they continued on, buoyed by their determination and encouraged by their convictions.

Thus, it is to these pioneer women we offer our praise and gratitude. We acknowledge their rightful recognition and appreciation as we look back into history and realize how far we have come into the world of accomplishment and recognition.

It is a little-known fact that:

a woman printed the Declaration of Independence;

Mary Ann Lee was the first American dancer, at age 12, to bring the beauty and poetry of romantic ballet to her country on the stage of Philadelphia's Chestnut Theater in 1838;

the first women's United States bank opened in 1919 in Clarksville, Tennessee, with (of course) a staff comprised of all women;

the first female telegrapher placed her hand on the key-signal at Lowell, Massachusetts, Telegraph Depot on February 21, 1846;

the first young woman to win a Miss America title was a high school sophomore who later, during the financially devastating years of the Great Depression, found it necessary to melt down her silver trophies in order to meet her household expenses;

at age 33, Lucy Taylor became the first woman to graduate from the Ohio College of Dental Surgery in Cincinnati in 1866, although her diploma read "To Gentleman Graduate . . ." She was the pioneer woman about whom was said, "She is a young girl who has so forgotten her womanhood as to want to study dentistry."

the first woman to be pictured on U.S. currency (the one-dollar bill) was Martha Washington in 1886;

the first female candidates to take the NASA entry exam scored so well that the exams were discontinued . . . officials simply were not prepared to accept a woman into the U.S. space program.

"The First of the First" occurred on August 18, 1587, when Virginia Dare (the daughter of Ellinor White and Ananias Dare) became the first child of English parents to be born on American soil. Virginia's grandfather (Virginia Colony Governor John White) returned to England only 9 days after his granddaughter's birth and, when he returned to the colony three years later, found that nothing remained of the early settlement.

Giving birth on the ground is oftentimes difficult enough, but doing so at high altitudes often complicates matters even more. Mrs. T.W. Evans was the first American woman to give birth in an airplane (in 1929) while flying over Miami, Florida.

Full-term infants face enough risks, but "early arriving bundles" face even greater obstacles, even in today's world of advanced medical technology. Imagine the scenario when tiny Edith Eleanor McLean weighed in at only two pounds and seven ounces when she arrived two months prematurely at the State Emigrant Hospital at Ward's Island in New York City in 1888. This author could find no record of what became of little Edith after her arrival.

Giving birth to one's own children is note-worthy in itself, but to give birth to one's own GRANDCHILDREN is certainly the talk of the town, or the state, or the country, or the world! Arlett Rafferty, Schweitzer's daughter (Christa Schweitzer Uchytil) was unable to bear children. In 1991 (at age 43), as an act of love, Arlett agreed to carry and bear the twin boy and girl that were the fertilized embryos of her daughter and son-in-law. The only other similar case of motherly love comes out of South Africa, where a woman gave birth to her daughter's triplets in 1987.

Mary Ann and Andrew Fischer, a South Dakota farming couple in their 30s, lived on a small farm where they were raising their five children on Andrew's shipping clerk's take-home pay of less than eighty dollars per week, the food from their farm, and the milk from their two cows. As Mary Ann waited to give birth for the sixth time, their family obviously was about to increase. But they had not anticipated the rapid growth their family was about to experience! On September 14, 1963, Mary Ann Fischer became the first U.S. woman to successfully give birth to quintuplets! In addition to the family's five children, four girls and one boy joined the ranks. As the news spread around the world, the Fishers became known as the family of **7** who had, within a matter of moments, suddenly become the family of **12**!

Part II - The World of Business and Finance

Victoria Woodhull was born in 1838 in the small town of Homer, Ohio. At the age of 32, she (along with her sister) opened the brokerage firm of Woodhull, Chafin, and Company on Wall Street in 1870. The sisters became known as "bold and successful operators on the Street," despite the initial claims by their male counterparts that . . . being such fascinating and fashionably dressed ladies of their times . . . they could not possibly be shrewd speculators. Although the sisters' commissions totaled only one-eighth of one percent, they managed to earn 500 dollars in comissions on sales during a particular 11-day period. Ultimately known as "The Fanciful Financier," Miss Woodhull was successful in carrying out other advances for women . . . including the founding of the Women's International Agricultural Club, joining of the Ladies' Automobile Club, the organization of the Women's Aerial League of England, and the offering of five thousand dollars to the first transatlantic aviator.

Susan B. Anthony, women's suffragist, was the first female to be pictured on a U.S. coin in 1979. U.S. Treasury officials also considered Nellie Tayloe Ross (first woman governor from Wyoming in 1924), Jane Addams (first female Nobel Peace Prize winner in 1860), and Eleanor Roosevelt (U.S. First Lady).

Sarah Breedlove Walker, daughter of sharecropping parents in the Louisiana Delta during the mid 1800s, was a mother and widow before the age of twenty. She had been supporting herself and her child by taking in laundry for a daily fee of $1.50 when she decided there had to be a better way of life. She created a complete line of hair products for black women, soon outgrowing her working space within her home. Having opened factories in Denver and Pittsburgh, she soon employed over three thousand people. In 1908, Sarah married Charles Walker, a newspaperman, and began referring to herself as Madame C.J. Walker;

by 1914, she was a millionaire who never forgot her humble beginnings . . . contributing to many charities for the remainder of her life.

During the 1700s, Mary Katherine Goddard was publisher of the *Providence* [Rhode Island] *Gazette,* and Mary managed to keep her paper afloat during the Revolutionary War when other papers were being forced out of business. Being not only an expert editor but also an excellent typographer, she accepted outside jobs to help supplement her income. In 1775, Mary accepted the position of postmaster of the Annapolis-Baltimore postal station, thereby becoming the first American woman to hold that position. The following year, members of Congress asked Miss Goddard to print copies of the **Declaration of Independence** so that citizens in every state could have access to the document.

Laura Keene, born in London, England, in the early 1800s, arrived in New York City to make her stage debut in 1852. Only three years later, she opened her own theater where she became manager and leading lady. She is known as the theater personality who established the matinee as a regular feature of theater life. Laura had spent her brightest days in the theater, and history would reveal that she would spend her darkest day in the theater also. She was in Ford's Theater the night Abraham Lincoln was shot and found herself holding the head of the United States President in her lap until he was taken from the theater to the home across the street where he subsequently died.

Part III - The World of Medicine

In the mid 1800s, Emeline Roberts Jones began learning the field of dentistry as an assistant to her dentist-husband in Danielsville, Connecticut. After four years of working closely with him, she became his official partner and continued to run the practice after his death. Since a degree in dentistry was not a requirement for practicing in the dental field at that time in history, "Dr. Emeline" encountered no legal obstacles and began specializing in treatment for women and children.

Later in the 1800s, however, a dentistry degree *was* required to practice, and Lucy Beaman Hobbs (having been refused admission to medical school because of her gender) gave up her career in education to pursue dentistry. Having become proficient in dental procedures and the administering of anesthesia, Lucy applied to the Ohio College of Dental Surgery in 1861. Sadly, history repeated itself, and Lucy again found herself being denied admission because of her gender. Having moved to Iowa and winning the respect of her colleagues, the Iowa Dental Society granted her membership in 1865. After she achieved that recognition, she received acceptance to the state's dental college. Recognizing that Lucy had accumulated the extensive amount of training and expertise in her desired field of endeavor, the college granted her degree after only four months of training. Upon graduation, she married and moved to Kansas where she began teaching her new husband enough dentistry that he eventually became a partner in her practice.

Strange as it may seem, the first medical school (1848) and medical society for women were begun by a man . . . Samuel Gregory. The Female Medical Educational Society (which would later become part of the Boston University School of Medicine) set as its purpose to "provide and promote the education of midwives, nurses, and female physicians and to diffuse among women generally a knowledge of physiology and the principles and means of preserving and restoring health."

And during the school's and society's years of struggle for establishment and recognition, Elizabeth Blackwell was involved in her own personal struggle . . . that of being admitted to a recognized school of medicine. Having *applied* at . . . and being *rejected* at . . . twenty-nine schools, while simultaneously being harassed and ridiculed for her dreams and attempts. Elizabeth was finally accepted at the Medical Institute at Geneva, New York. She had crossed a huge hurdle, but all of Elizabeth's difficult times were not in the past. Upon admission, she was not permitted to attend classroom demonstrations of procedures, she was cursed and spat upon, and was initially denied housing. But she persevered, ultimately graduated at the top of her class, and opened the New York Infirmary for Women and Children (staffed entirely by women). She later went to England, where she helped found the London School of Medicine for Women. She died in 1910 at the age of eighty-nine.

In 1870, Dr. Susan Steward became the first black physician, graduating from the New York Medical College for Women as valedictorian of her class. Upon completion of her studies, she opened a family practice in Brooklyn, where she treated both black and white patients. During the next forty years, Dr. Steward practiced her beloved medicine, married twice, and raised her family.

Shortly after he took office in 1961, President John F. Kennedy appointed the first female White House physician, Dr. Janet Travell (who had previously been Kennedy's personal physician).

Part IV - The World of Aviation

As women were experiencing difficulty pursuing their dreams while walking upon the earth, there were courageous and adventuresome women who dreamed of taking to the skies. As humankind was marveling at the Wright Brothers and their attempt to fly as birds, Mrs. Hart Berg, whose husband was the Wrights' European representative, took a two-minute flight with Wilbur Wright at Auvers, France, in 1908. To avoid having her clothing becoming caught in the plane's controls, Mrs. Berg tied her hat onto her head with a scarf and her full skirt around her ankles with a cord. Upon her landing, Mrs. Berg received little attention from the French press as being the first woman to fly, but because she failed to untie her skirt before walking away from the aircraft, French designers created a line of new fashion which was referred to as the "hobble skirt."

It would be several years later, in 1914, when a woman would become the first female passenger on a regularly scheduled airline flight. After being in service only one week, a Florida-based line shuttled Mrs. L.A. Whitney from St. Petersburg to Tampa, a ten-mile trip that would forever place her name in the annals of history of "female firsts."

The first female flight attendants, known as the Flying Florence Nightingales, were all registered nurses. The pioneer of this endeavor, Miss Ellen Church, persuaded Air Transport, a predecessor of United Airlines, to hire her as chief stewardess, where she quickly recruited seven other women who met required standards . . . single, no older than 25, weighing less than 115 pounds, and no taller than 5-foot-4 . . . at a monthly salary of $125 for 100 flying hours. Miss Church revealed her insight into human nature when she first persuaded Air Transport to hire women by observing that it would be good psychology to have a woman flying in the air by asking, "How is a man going to say he is afraid to fly when a woman is working on the plane?" The historic flight occurred on May 15, 1930, when the first four attendants flew the first leg of the flight from San Francisco to Cheyenne, Wyoming; the remaining four stewardesses cared for the passengers on the second leg from Cheyenne to Chicago, Illinois.

The first black airline attendant, a nurse from Ithaca, New York, made history in 1957, when she flew for Mohawk Airlines (which would later become part of Allegheny Airlines) between Ithaca and New York City.

On Independence Day, 1880, Mary H. Myers became America's first woman balloonist at Little Falls, New York. Six years later, she reached the astonishing altitude of four miles in a balloon filled with natural gas. Her skill and accuracy exercised in her landings brought her recognition, particularly in lieu of the fact that her balloon was not equipped with oxygen. Her love of ballooning was revealed during the next thirty years, during which time she and her husband did extensive studies in designing portable hydrogen generators, improving balloon fabrics, inventing a method for steering for which she received a patent, and experimenting with light-weight automobiles.

The first female U.S. astronaut candidate to be tested was Jerrie Cobb, a 29-year-old pilot from Oklahoma in 1959. While such recognized men as John Glenn and Alan Shepard were being publically tested, Jerrie was being *secretly* tested. During the next three years, twenty-four women were also tested. Although all of them scored high on their evaluations (sometimes receiving scores high than Glenn's) and were rated "excellent" in their space flight suitability, NASA suddenly suspended all testing on women. Only under a congressional subcommittee's questioning did NASA admit they simply were not prepared to have a woman represent their country in the space program. They were merely experimenting with the idea, perhaps preparing for a future time during which women might be accepted into such a pioneering program. But another nation was making pioneering strides into space, and another woman, Valentina Tereshkova of the Soviet Union, became the first woman to make a flight into outer space in 1963.

It was not until 1978 that NASA announced its first six female candidates selected for training. Although none of the women would be permitted to pilot the spacecraft, they would assist in all operational activities and in carrying out research projects aboard the craft while in space. The six candidates included:

> Katherine Sullivan, a geologist from Cupertino, California;
>
> Dr. Anna Fisher, a physician from Rancho Palos Verdes, California;
>
> Shannon Lucid, a biochemist from Oklahoma City;
>
> Judith Resnick, an electrical engineer from Akron, Ohio;
>
> Sally Ride, a physics researcher from Stanford University;
>
> Dr. Margaret Seddon, a surgeon from Memphis, Tennessee.

Part V - The World of Politics and Law

The first woman to be recognized as a lawyer was Arabella Babb Mansfield who graduated from Iowa Wesleyan University in 1866. After a three-year apprenticeship, she took the Iowa bar exam, along with her husband and several other men, and was credited with achieving high honors. One can only imagine her disappointment and frustration when she learned that she would not automatically be admitted to the bar, for the statute stipulated that only "white males" would be eligible. Later that year, however, a judge ruled that Mrs. Mansfield was, indeed, eligible for membership within the Iowa Bar Association, and she was duly accepted. The following year, the term "white males" was removed from the statute. Interestingly enough, Mrs. Mansfield never practiced law, for she soon entered graduate school, studying in both England and France. She later returned to Iowa and became a law professor.

During the 1870s, Belva Lockwood sought admission to two law schools but was denied admittance because of her gender. The National University Law School in Washington, DC., permitted her to complete all necessary course work but would not grant her a degree until President Ulysses S. Grant intervened. Later, as she attempted to argue her first case before the U.S. Supreme Court, she was again denied permission because of her gender, being told that it was "not the custom" for a woman to do so. Refusing to be defeated, Lockwood lobbied Congress and was primarily responsible for the eventual passage of a bill that granted such rights to women. Continuing to practice law, she argued her last case before the Supreme Court in 1907 (at age seventy-six) in which she gained a five million dollar settlement for the Eastern Cherokee Indians.

As the number of women lawyers increased, the need for a women's group to promote the interest of women lawyers was quickly realized. In 1899, a group of women lawyers practicing law in Connecticut, New Jersey, and New York City formed the Women Lawyers' Club which was renamed the Women Lawyers' Association nine years later.

Few individuals, if asked, would realize that the first woman presidential candidate was Victoria Claflin Woodhull who began her endeavors in 1838 in New York City.

Ella Tambusii Grasso (the daughter of Italian immigrants) became the first woman to be elected a U.S. governor who did not succeed her husband into office. She also holds the distinction of being the first woman to be re-elected to such a position. In 1975, Grasso won in a landslide victory against her opponent

Jeannette Rankin of Montana was the first Congresswoman to be elected to the U.S. House of Representatives in 1916. She lost her bid for re-election, and many people believed her defeat was brought about by her outspoke anti-war sentiments. She was the only state representative who cast a dissenting vote to officially declare the start of World War I. Rankin continued her work for women's rights during the next twenty years, and she was returned to the senate in 1940 (where she remained until 1943). Rankin holds the distinction of being the only member of Congress to vote *twice* against the U.S. entering into war (both for World Wars I and II).

Part VI - The World of Arts and Entertainment

Nearly every living human has fond memories of going to the circus, and perhaps the fondest of those memories is seeing the clowns in all their colorful, klutzy antics. And, most likely, as we returned home, we dreamed of becoming one of those loveable characters ourselves. Clowns have been part of even our earliest human history when they appeared in the royal circles as "court jesters." But what kind of person would make a good clown?

Peggy Williams made clown history in 1970 when she became the first female clown after graduating from the Ringling Brothers and Barnum & Bailey Circus Clown College in Venice, Florida. Williams, a 21-year-old speech therapist from Wisconsin, had attended the college to learn more about non-verbal communication (which she planned to use in her practice). However, during her training, she came to believe that she could accomplish more from "inside a circus ring than from inside a clinic" and therefore changed the direction of her endeavors.

Elsie de Wolfe, who had become known during the late 1800s for her acting ability and her distinguished good taste in matters of appearance, was commissioned in 1905 to decorate The Colony Club (New York City's first club exclusively for women). Her decorative talents utilized the introduction of multiple mirrors, brightly colored fabrics, table lamps, and the running of electrical cords inside walls.

The first female syndicated cartoon columnist was Dale Messic who created the "Brenda Starr" comic strip in 1940. Fearing that newspaper editors would refuse to accept her work if they realized she was a woman, she changed her name to Dale from its original "Dalia." And, thus, "Brenda Starr," the first comic strip to have a female lead character, appeared for its premier run on June 19, 1940, in the Chicago *Tribune*.

Turning to the visual news media, Dorothy Fuldheim is credited with being the first woman news anchorwoman. She truly was fighting a battle that no woman had fought before and, as she stepped before the television cameras in 1947, in Cleveland, Ohio, her heart must surely have been racing. However, the spot's sponsor reacted negatively and insisted that a man must have the position. But the station stood behind its promise to Fuldheim and, as her popularity among listeners grew, the original sponsor returned and continued their sponsorship for the next eighteen years. Dorothy was still at her anchorwoman's desk in 1979 when, at age eighty-six, she became the longest-running television broadcaster . . . male *or* female.

Janet Gaynor made headlines when, in 1937, she won an Academy Award for best acting. With the release of *The Johnstown Flood, Seventh Heaven,* and *Sunrise*, Gaynor became Fox Studio's top star.

Theda Bara shocked the "silent movies" viewing world in 1914 by becoming the first actress to wear eye make-up (created by cosmetics tycoon Helena Rubenstein) for the production of *A Fool There Was.*

Movie-goers were astonished to see May Irwin become the first woman to share an on-screen kiss with co-star John Rice in the film, *The Widow Jones*, in 1896. After all, such public displays of affection were frowned upon at that point in history.

Bette Davis was perhaps best known for her starring roles in *Dangerous, Jezebel, All About Eve, The Man Who Played God, Of Human Bondage*, and *Strangers: The Story of a Mother and a Daughter.* But Davis' "first woman" achievement came with being named the head of the Academy of Motion Picture Arts and Sciences in 1941. She was also the first to receive the Film Institute's highest honor . . . the Life Achievement Award . . . in 1977. With such accomplishments *to* her credit, it is a bit ironic that her autobiography, released in 1962, was titled *The Lonely Life.*

From Carol's Rose Garden

. . . about

OTHER THINGS

Bridges, Bridges . . . Everywhere Bridges

What is a bridge? Is it something that separates? Or is it something that joins?

There are all types of bridges, made from all types of materials.

Wooden bridges.

Rope bridges.

Metal bridges.

Bridges with canopy tops.

Bridges with no tops.

Bridges with short side railings.

Bridges with tall side railings.

Bridges with see-through bottoms.

There are short bridges.

And long bridges.

Bridges that have stood steady for decades.

And bridges that have buckled and collapsed under excessive weight or during natural disasters.

Some individuals fear bridges and will shut their eyes when crossing them (assuming they are not driving a vehicle). Some people have such a deep-seated fear of bridges that they will go to any extreme to keep from crossing them altogether. But other individuals feel a sense of flight and power as they find themselves suspended over canyons, valleys, and rivers.

A story appeared in the media many years ago of a community that decided to paint their bridge *red* for some unknown reason. It was not long before the "powers that be" realized what a terrible error they had made. Since the repainting of the bridge to that bright, emotional color of red, the rate of suicides from its railings had increased several-fold. Realizing this, the city fathers immediately had the span repainted again . . . this time to a very neutral color. And the suicide rate dropped dramatically.

There are bridges that bring us together . . . when we develop more meaningful and honest communication, when we experience similar circumstances as those people around us have experienced, or when we gain additional insight into human behavior.

But the hardest bridge of all to cross is the one that opens our hearts, for we often fear self-revelation. We fear that such exposure will make us vulnerable, and that others will see traits in us we would rather keep hidden.

Oh, that each of us could realize how this fear of opening our heart to those around us robs us of such potential blessings and marvelous encounters!

Bottomless Wells of Love

LOVE . . . a four-letter word most us use every day.

All of us know what it means. We have heard it since the days of our infancy. But stop for just a moment . . . before going further, let your mind wander and see if you can put the definition for *LOVE* into words. . . . .

Webster defines it as "a deep and tender feeling of affection for or attachment or devotion to a person or persons."

We see love all around us.

Or do we?

Is it the *love* we are seeing, or is it the outward *manifestations* of love?

Love is like the wind. We cannot see it, but we certainly experience its effects. Love has been the topic of poems, stories, music, books, greeting cards, and media coverage since the beginning of time. But perhaps the word has been so excessively used that it has lost some of its intent. We say that we *l-o-v-e* everything from our most precious loved ones to baseball and apple pie.

Love is innate in all of us. No one taught us to love. We did it naturally as infants in our parents' arms. We were not instructed on the fine points of cuddling, snuggling, and desiring those warm "fuzzies." We did it naturally. We desired that warm, safe feeling of protection and assurance from our very first hours on Earth.

As we matured, we realized that love does not ask how much we **must** do, but rather how much we **can** do. Someone once said interest will begin a hard work. Determination will continue it.

But only love makes us endure to the end. We are able to give without loving, but we cannot love without giving.

Many relationships have begun because of kind deeds or words. And many close relationships . . . husbands and wives, mothers and fathers, brothers and sisters . . . have been destroyed because of hurtful or hateful words spoken in haste. Perhaps that is why animals make such wonderful pets . . . they wag their tails and not their tongues.

We have frequently been reminded that fools rush in where angels fear to tread. But there is another group of individuals who also rush in where angels fear to tread . . . parents . . . not hesitating to face all dangers and threats in protecting their children. Such action is borne out of love. And how do children and love relate?

Merely look into the faces of young children as they watch the world around them. Watch as they immediately trust anyone they encounter.

Children radiate love. They appear to be the very essence of love (most times)! They seem to simultaneously *soak up* and *pour out* unconditional love. And such love is not based upon material possessions or social standing or prominent addresses or positions of power and authority. It is based upon a God-given need to love and *be* loved.

Nothing is stronger than the bond of love between parents and their children. We, as adults, must realize that each child is a bottomless well of love. And we must tap into it.

Go to School, Kill the Spirit

Perhaps the worst thing we do to our children is send them to school. We take those precious, lively, vivid imaginations and stuff them into our one-dimensional educational boxes. We tell them to be quiet, to sit up straight, to hold their pencil a certain way, to put their paper at the proper angle, and to put their feet flat on the floor. We tell them that 9:00 a.m. is the proper time for learning math, and that 2:00 p.m. is the proper time for learning English. We believe we must never rearrange the schedule, or we will create uncertainty in their world.

We tell them to walk **to** the restroom on the *right* side of the hallway and to walk **from** the restroom on the *left* side of the hallway. We teach them to keep their desks in straight rows. We tell them that ducks should be colored yellow, and that pigs should be colored pink. We instruct them to put their **names** on the *left* side of the paper, and to put the **date** on the *right* side of the paper.

Now please understand . . . as a former classroom teacher, I am not advocating "kid freedom" in our learning institutions. We know that would result in nothing but chaos and little or no learning. What I am suggesting is that we recognize and appreciate the beautiful imaginative minds and spirits kids have . . . and to allow them to *use* those enterprising and fertile spirits.

We, as adults, need to have fun with children's magical worlds of creativeness. Treat yourself to a wonderful experience and sit down with a child. Ask that child to think about the following questions, and you will be wonderfully amazed at the answers you may receive:

Which is smarter . . . a carrot or a pumpkin?

What would happen if cows started producing orange juice instead of milk?

What would happen if rain fell *up* instead of *down*?

What would we do if puppies meowed and kittens barked?

Why aren't bananas orange?

How would we feel if someone served us green mashed potatoes?

How would we feel if we were a dollar bill?

How are a balloon and a marshmallow alike?

What do we think our favorite stuffed animal would say to us?

What would we say to a dinosaur?

How would we feel if we were a kite on a windy day?

What kind of games do fish play?

How are a snowflake and a raindrop alike?

What would we do if we were a train?

What do the clothes in our closet say to each other?

What problem would we talk about to the President?

Engage in activities that you and your child can enjoy together . . . that allow you as an adult to relax and enjoy being a kid again such as:

Blowing bubbles

Planting a garden

Playing in a nearby creek

Looking for wildflowers

Fingerpainting

Visiting the zoo

Reading a joke book

Watching the stars twinkle

Talking to a favorite pet

Flying paper airplanes

Remember that your children, whether they are *two* or *twenty-two,* are your future. They are your legacy that you leave to the world. They are your investment in eternity.

And, realizing their vital importance, love them, spend time with them, and treat them accordingly . . . as you would any other priceless possession.

Life is not a dress rehearsal. It is the real thing.

And we will *live* with . . . and *die* with . . . the decisions we make . . . the decisions we make **today.**

From Barbie Dolls to Lug Nuts

It all began as the 1969 Camaro arrived in our driveway. Our daughter Sarah had purchased the eye-sore with the small inheritance she had received from her great-grandfather's estate. My husband Dave is an Automobile Collision and Repair Technology instructor at Prosser School of Technology in New Albany, Indiana. He had previously inspected the car and decided that it would make a wonderful restoration project to be presented to Sarah as a high school graduation gift in four years. Due to the estimated cost involved, however, we reminded our daughter that it must also serve as a gift for college graduation, wedding, and first baby!

After forking over $400.00 to the elderly original owners, a few small details needed attention . . . airing up the four flat tires, filling an empty transmission, sweeping out the cobwebs, charging the battery, and adding one quart of oil. The original garnet-colored paint had faded into a deep purple mess, and the interior was torn and badly stained from nicotine.

Over the next four years, Sarah's "first love" received two new quarter panels, outer wheel housings, front fenders, header panel, core support, and cowl induction hood. The original drum brakes were replaced with new power disc units, and a Muncie four-speed transmission with a Hurst Competition Plus shifter took the place of the 350 turbo automatic. The original suspension was trashed, and Z-28 suspension components were installed.

The ten-bolt 3:08 single trac rear end was traded for a twelve-bolt posi trac with 3:73 gears. The original two-barrel 350 engine was completely rebuilt and mildly modified to include a .030 over bore, mild Competition Cam shaft, original Z-28 intake, and four-barrel carburetor.

All chrome was replaced with genuine GM parts. The interior was recovered using late model GM cloth and vinyl material. The exterior was sprayed with 1990 Chevrolet Red, and white rally stripes were added. Corvette 15x8 rally rims were placed in the rear, and 15x7 rims were placed up front. Four 245/60x15 tires completed the package.

During the restoration process, Sarah helped her dad cut off the old quarter panels with an air chisel, helped reinstall the subframe, front suspension, and rear end. Other times, she assisted in the clean-up responsibilities, and offered a helping hand when *another* hand was needed.

The Camaro made its debut on the show scene in late 1992 and has since taken two trophies from Carl Casper's International Car Show, in addition to many other first and second place trophies from area cruises and competitions. Sarah's "first love" has also been featured in Posie's Pick in *Hot Rod Magazine*, *The Courier-Journal*, *Fun on Wheels* (a nation-wide show car magazine), and *Super Chevy*.

When Sarah first began competing in 1992 at the age of 18, she suffered many negative comments from males as they praised the vehicle. Such comments included the following: "No. Cars like this don't belong to girls" "What's a girl doing with a car like this?" and "I'll bet you don't know anything about it." They were shocked when she began rattling off the specs and could answer their specific questions. She took delight in proving that females CAN and DO, indeed, know about their automobiles.

The car is protected with a burglar alarm system, covered while kept in the garage, and driven only in good weather. Preparing for larger competitions involves extensive engine compartment cleaning, hand-rubbing the complete undercarriage (including everything from main frame rails to springs), vacuuming complete interior and carpeted trunk, using Q-tips and Armor-All to clean tires AND TREAD, polishing windows with window cleaner and newspaper, and applying 2-3 coats of polish to all metal parts.

Many individuals have inquired about purchasing the Camaro, but Sarah has declined all offers. One gentleman, having attempted to buy the car on several occasions, finally said in desperation, "What do you want for the car? Everything has a price tag!"

Sarah responded rather indignantly, "Not this car. It's not for sale. My dad spent four years of his life building this car just for me, and I'm not selling it." Case closed!

I am sure Sarah was not consciously aware of the reaons behind her decision . . . how a closer relationship between herself and her dad had developed during the restroation process; how her dad had given so freely of *himself* so he could give his daughter a tangible gift of his love for her; how a father had gained insight into his daughter, and how (simultaneously) a daughter had gained insight into her father.

In case one wonders what our daughter does for daily transportation, since the Camaro is certainly not a daily-driver, she can be seen scouting the countryside in her 1985 CJ-7 Jeep.

Epilogue:

Nothing in life is static and neither was this situation. Since the original writing of this article, Sarah has graduated from college, become a professional career woman, sold her Camaro and Jeep, purchased a sporty new car and put the remainder of the money in the bank toward the purchase of her first home.

Young People's Greatest Resource: Older Folks' Wisdom

Is has often been said that energy is wasted on the young, and wisdom is wasted on the old. How sad. But how true. As the energy of youth seems to know no limits, would it not be more fair to graciously grant some of that vim, vigor, and vitality to members of the older generation? Could it not help ease the older folks' sufferings as they endure the maladies of aging bodies? Would they not rejoice in the thrill of renewed stamina and vitality? Sadly enough, such a gift is not usually given. We cannot physically transfuse stimulating enterprise from one individual to another. To a great degree, the lost dynamic energy of youth is lost forever.

Or is it?

Is it not possible to keep the energy of youth through a forever-young spirit and perspective? Is it not possible to preserve that magical wonder as the body ages? Is there not a difference between aging and growing old? Aging is an inevitable fact of life. But growing old . . . that can frequently be a matter of choice and of mind. Could it be said that age is merely a perception . . . that, as Victor Hugo once observed, "Forty is the old age of youth, while fifty is the youth of old age"?

Oliver Wendell Holmes, American writer of the 1800s, once observed that to be seventy years old is sometimes far more cheerful than to be forty years old. Thus, perhaps the greatest pain of maturing is losing one's zest for life . . . of forgetting the magic of a sunset . . . of neglecting to smell the flowers . . . of failing to pet a friendly dog . . . of being inattentive to falling leaves . . *of slipping into oblivion.*

The youthful fools tell the world what they will do, while the boastful middle-agers brag of what they have accomplished. But the wise individuals . . . they are the achievers who accomplish their tasks and say nothing. And thus the difference between knowledge and wisdom . . . knowledge being proud of learning so much, and wisdom being humble of knowing no more. And as Alfred, Lord Tennyson so eloquently phrased it long ago, "Knowledge comes, but wisdom lingers."

An Arab philosopher once decided:

There are four kinds of people:

Those who know not,

and know not that they know not.

They are foolish.

Those who know not,

and know they know not.

These are the simple, and should be instructed.

Those who know,

and know not that they know.

They are asleep. Wake them.

Those who know,

and know they know.

They are the wise. Listen to them.

Perhaps the greatest gift that older folks can bestow upon the younger generation is the realization that true wisdom is seeing the miracles of common, everyday life. And as the poet William Wordsworth reminded, "Wisdom is oftentimes nearer when we *stoop* than when we *soar*."

One of the greatest gifts we can bestow upon ourselves is to spend time with a silver-haired soul . . . an individual who has walked the stony path of life and has learned its lessons. One who has experienced both joy and pain, and talks of the value of both. One who has insight into some of life's greatest mysteries, yet marvels at the sparkle in a child's innocent eyes. One who has learned to laugh with those who are joyful, to weep with those who are sorrowing, and to be silent with those who are questioning . . . realizing that silence will often cause those who are asking to find their own answers.

Develop a respect for the mature and the elderly. Take a marvelous journey into life with one who has lived the yesterdays, enjoys the todays, and anticipates the tomorrows. And when you complete your travel, you will have gained a deeper perspective into this thing we call LIFE.

Through These Halls

As I sit in the waiting area of a local university, I am aware of individuals passing through these halls. They appear in a variety of sizes, shapes, and colors . . . and each student has his or her own style of arrival.

Some students shuffle along at a snail-like pace, and I wonder about their motivation and true interest in their current course of studies. Their outward appearance makes the casual observer believe they are totally unconcerned about such matters. Is this a true indication of their inner attitudes, or is it a facade they feel they must present to the world?

Others arrive with such a fast-paced stride, I wonder what is encouraging them to rush to class. Is it a sincere desire to be punctual so as not to miss any important academic information? Or is it a wish to visit with fellow classmates before class? Or is it merely a desire to avoid being noticed by the professor as they arrive late for lecture?

A majority of the younger students pass through these halls with a spring in their step that would indicate a sense of lightness and freedom from care. Perhaps they are feeling the joy of youth that focuses upon future goals and dreams. Are they being propelled by their anticipation of what awaits them?

Many of the older students that arrive seem to be burdened by a heavy load. Are they oppressed by the physical slowing brought about by increasing age? Is their burden compounded by caring for their younger children, trying teenagers, or aging parents? Perhaps they are struggling with financial obligations and are fearful that there will be too much month left at the end of the money. Perhaps they are coping with current job frustrations or a job change that requires further education . . . and they are concerned over their ability to compete with the younger students.

As we consider this matter of universities, course studies,

and learning, we suddenly realize there are certain criteria that designates a person as a true thinker.

In *The Book of Lists*, Will Durant lists whom he considers to be the nine greatest thinkers of all time. We may, or may not, agree with these thinkers' views. And, of course, our own views would determine whether or not we thought a particular person was a great thinker. But as we consider these individuals' contributions to the world of thought, perhaps we should ask ourselves if our present-day society has not somehow lost the appreciation for those persons who spend quality time in deep contemplation about themselves and the world around them.

Confucius (551? B.C. - 479? B.C.) Chinese philosopher

Plato (427? - 347 B.C.) Greek philosopher

Aristotle (384-322 B.C.) Greek philosopher

St. Thomas Aquinas (1125-1274) Italian theologian

Nicolaus Copernicus (1473-1543) Polish astronomer

Francis Bacon (1561-1626) English statesman and philosopher

Sir Isaac Newton (1642-1727) English mathematician and physicist

Voltaire (1694-1778) French author

Immanuel Kant (1724-1804) German philosopher

Have we, perhaps, come to a point in human history when consideration, contemplation, and consultation are no longer considered important. Have we become a society of followers, choosing to take the path of least resistance, merely going with the flow?

We may find it *interesting*, and likely ***frightening***, to know that Roget's Thesaurus lists only one antonym (opposite meaning) for the word "THOUGHT" . . . and it is "STUPIDITY."

This Thing Called Time

As we were driving home from church one Sunday, our son Mark, who was 7 years old at the time, shattered our complacency with the question "Mom, when time passes, where does it go?"

Now, truthfully, have *you* ever thought of that? I hadn't.

And in my maternal desire to give my son an answer of some true content, yet not boggle his mind more than he had already boggled mine, I asked a wise and trusted friend (and father of four sons) for some assistance. With the question repeated, he calmly looked at me and quietly said, "Tell him that it passes from this earth and becomes part of God's eternity." I thought that was a pretty good answer. It also satisfied Mark. But then I began to be concerned over the *next* profound question he would ask and wondered if I would be better prepared for that one. After all, I was an adult, and I had never thought of such a question!

After the initial shock of a child asking such a thought-provoking question, I began to think about this thing called time. What is it . . . really? Stop for just a moment and ask yourself to define that little four-letter word TIME.

If you will check a good dictionary, you will most likely be surprised to see the number of definitions that are listed. But, basically, time is considered as "an indefinite, unlimited duration in which things are considered as happening in the past, present, or future . . . every moment there has ever been or ever will be."

We live in a very time oriented society. We have clocks in our offices, and clocks throughout our homes. We wear them on our wrists, we wear them on our fingers (yes, there are finger watches), we wear them on chains around our necks, and we have them in our automobiles. A recent report revealed that the average American looked at his or her watch an average of 300 times per day!

What are we watching?

What are we waiting for?

When we were children and our parents were attempting to teach us patience, they would often quote the old adage, "Everything comes to him who waits." But as adults, we realized that the one thing that will *not* come to those who wait is the precious time lost while waiting.

The following is a piece of advice that appeared in the *Hawkinsville Dispatch News* many years ago:

TAKE TIME

Take time to work — it is the price of success.

Take time to think — it is the source of power.

Take time to play — it is the secret of perpetual youth.

Take time to read — it is the foundation of wisdom.

Take time to worship — it is the highway to reverence.

Take time to be friendly — it is the road to happiness.

Take time to dream — it is hitching one's wagon to a star.

Take time to love and be loved — it is the privilege of life.

Take time to live — it is the secret of success.

Take time to laugh — it helps lift life's load.

Take time to pray — it brings God near and washes the dust of earth from our eyes.

No conscientious soul would advocate squandering time, of course, for wisdom tells us that the most extravagant and costly of all expenses is the wasting of time. Yet, simultaneously, we must realize that we simply cannot erase leisure time from our lives. We must never equate wasting time with leisure time, for our bodies are designed to require time away from tasks in order to keep a proper perspective on our responsibilities.

But as we evaluate our current way of life in today's society, has it ever struck us odd that Americans have more time-saving devices and less free time than any other country in the world? What should that say to us? That perhaps the individuals who make the best use of their time have the most to spare?

Thus, the final question we must ask is this: "Is time something that is measured in hours and days, or is it something that is measured in *love* and *relationships* . . . those things that somehow transcend the boundaries of time?"

The After-Christmas Wreckage

It was three days after Christmas, and I decided that it was now safe to venture into the stores to look for bargains. I attempted doing this in years past on the very day after Christmas, but the animalistic behavior of fellow-shoppers made me decide the trauma to my social graces and to my body had been too severe to consider doing such a foolish thing again.

As I wandered through the stores that day, I enjoyed the leisurely pace of the other shoppers surrounding me. They were not in a mad frenzy trying to find that perfect gift for Aunt Hilda, and Johnny and Janie were safe at home contentedly playing with their newly-possessed toys. I did see a few sad husbands being dragged along, displaying that pathetic "I'd rather be in the worst hospital in the city than here" look on their faces. Poor fellows, they did have my admiration. What we don't do in the name of love!

Strolling down the various aisles, I became acutely aware of what I suddenly realized was after-Christmas wreckage. And in the twinkling of an eye, I realized what I was seeing bore a striking resemblance to life itself.

On the shelves . . . Gone were the neatly stacked gift items and holiday decorations. Gone were the attractively wrapped consumer desires. Gone were the specially packaged goodies.

And in their place I found the following:

MISSING PRICE TAGS. How many times in our lives have we decided that we absolutely had to possess a certain object or achieve a certain goal, only to realize we could not find the price tag? But we weren't overly concerned. After all, it couldn't cost *that* much! And so we merrily began our quest, only to discover at a later time the price, indeed, was higher than we anticipated. Perhaps the expenditure was in dollars. Or more expensively, we found ourselves short-changed in time or energy or a relationship. Or perhaps the amount had been so exorbitant that we sacrificed our religious beliefs or our moral standards or our business ethics in the process of obtaining what we so desperately desired. And as we sat in utter despair, realizing that our dream had become our nightmare, we began asking ourselves, "Why didn't I look for the price tag?"

BROKEN TOYS WITH MISSING PARTS. When was the last time we took a thorough look at our lives, initially thinking that all was relatively well, only to discover that we were living only partial lives? Perhaps the peace within our home had been destroyed, or perhaps the contentment we had once known was absent. Perhaps in our fast-paced, get-all-you-can-get society, we laid aside our priorities.

Perhaps we continue to suffer the consequences of a fractured relationship. Or perhaps we are enduring the pain of severed communication with a loved one. As we sit amidst the debris, realizing that our lives are no longer complete, we begin asking ourselves, "Why didn't I work harder keeping the most important things in my life together?"

TORN PAPER. When did we last contemplate the ripped ties of a past friendship that ended during the trials of a misunderstanding? Perhaps the now-tattered connection was the result of a hurtful comment. Or a perceived lack of understanding. Or a felt sense of unequal give-and-take that is so terribly essential in all of our relationships. As we sit thinking about the ragged alliance we now suffer, we begin asking ourselves, "Was there something I could have done to mend that friendship or family alliance?"

CRUSHED TINSEL. When we evaluate our current circumstances, do we find those portions of our lives that were once the source of enjoyment and sparkle now lying bruised and trampled at our feet? Are we suddenly aware of the squashed people in our existence that we have carelessly beaten down in our frantic rush to gain, achieve, and prosper? Perhaps that original glow came from time spent with friends and loved ones. Perhaps it was the joy of taking time to appreciate nature at its fullest. Or perhaps it was simply the effort we took to look within ourselves and realize *who* and *what* we truly were. As we sit and contemplate the remnants of that which formerly brought us glowing glints of satisfaction, we begin asking ourselves, "Where did I begin to lose those vital links?"

MISSING INSTRUCTIONS. When we permit ourselves the opportunity to travel back in time throughout our learning experiences, what do we find? Do we realize that we oftentimes suffered unnecessary delays, hurts, and aggravations simply because we did not take the time or effort to seek the counsel of those older and wiser than ourselves? Did we endure additional frustrations because, in our youthful arrogance (or sometimes *older* arrogance), we considered ourselves worthy of knowing all the answers? Did we somehow feel that asking for assistance was a sign of weakness or lack of intelligence? As we sit and fully understand the ramifications of our actions, we begin asking ourselves, "Have I finally realized that I not only do not know all the *answers,* I have not even heard all the *questions* yet?"

EMPTY SHELVES. As we look at the supports that were once stocked with such things of beauty, attractiveness, and activity, we now see barren ledges of wood, metal, or plastic. Void of anything but space. The basic structure still remains, but the things that brought life and pleasure to the surroundings are suddenly gone. It seems that we are looking at another world, with nothing but a void staring back at us. And if we would be so brave as to look closely at our homes, would we find that same, empty void in them? Where we once heard laughter and watched relationships grow and flourish, do we now realize nothing but deafening quietness or artificial busyness? Not, perhaps, because the children are grown and gone. Not, perhaps, because loved ones have passed away. But because the warmth and love and interest and invested time we once gave have somehow been ignored or misplaced in our determination to achieve those thought-after and sought-after goals. As we stand and sadly realize our situation, we begin asking ourselves, "When did my *home* become a *house*?"

"ALL SALES FINAL" SIGNS. But perhaps the greatest ache of all comes with our realization that a portion of our lives has "finality" stamped upon them. Regardless of how deeply we regret certain thoughts or attitudes or actions, the stark reality cuts through us as a surgeon's knife that we cannot retrace our steps and undo the damage we have done. We may offer apologies. We may engage in deeds of kindness as an attempted act of repayment. We may promise ourselves that we learned a valuable lesson through the experience and will never make the same mistake again. But regardless of our soul-deep desire to go back and correct our wrong-doings, they are indelibly stamped upon the history books of our lives. There is no eraser large enough to eliminate the misfortune.

And, thus, we find ourselves at a crossroads. Do we choose to follow the path of regrets, self pity, and wishful thinking that creates illusions of how things "could have been"? Or do we make the conscious decision to turn toward the future . . . and the rest of our lives?

Yes, the future events of our tomorrows are uncertain, but we can take confidence in the fact that they will come only one day at a time. We must remember that our interest should be in the future, for we will spend the rest of our lives there. And although all of us carry things from our past we would like to change, we must also remember that we live in the present, dream of the future, and learn valuable and everlasting truths from our past.

Valued Workforce Members

The relationship between employer and employee has always been one of differing viewpoints, as each sees the situation from a personal, distinctive vantage point. But a recent report from the Kiplinger Washington editors sheds new intensive light on today's workforce situation and the future ramifications it holds for all American citizens.

Nationwide shortages among the labor force are spreading, particularly in the South, Midwest, and western mountain states. The situation is worse in the larger cities and suburbs, as opposed to small towns. In speaking with those individuals responsible for hiring, the news is that the shortages are reaching the critical stage.

Taking this shortage into account, many businesses and industries are fearful to implement expansion plans. Even worse, many businesses are turning away clients for lack of qualified workers. These companies' products or services simply cannot be delivered in proportion to the demand. And according to the established principle of supply and demand, the current workers are demanding a higher pay scale for their efforts and productivity. We see evidence of this principle by observing the higher wages and special incentive plans being offered.

Certain areas of employment are especially feeling the pressure of fewer workers and would deserve serious consideration by young people who are currently choosing their future vocations . . . computer programmers and analysts, software engineers and designers, skilled construction workers, welders, machinists, truck drivers, tool and die makers, auto mechanics, plumbers, repair technicians, sales clerks, electricians, and accountants.

In an attempt to correct this critical worker shortage, employers are implementing innovative programs that encourage both *recruitment* and *retention* of good workers. For companies realize that keeping good *present* workers is far better than locating and training *new* workers. Such "attracting" opportunities include the following:

Offering scholarships to students who commit to the company for future employment

Reviving apprenticeship programs whereby workers simultaneously combine learning and working

Increasing work-recruitment efforts on college campuses

Appealing to working couples by offering more flexible hours, thus enabling the spouses to more efficiently tend to personal responsibilities and obligations

Highlighting outstanding job performance, attendance records, and safety practices through worker recognition programs

Cooperating on matters of transportation, child care, and job training within the business

Offering bonuses to employees who recommend workers that are actually hired by the company

Hiring the more non traditional workers such as part-time and retired individuals, along with job-sharing partners

Recruiting from welfare rolls, overseas workers, and prison-release programs

If this current work crisis continues, every consumer in American will suffer the consequences . . . in higher wages which results in higher costs, in lower workforce numbers which results in reduced quality *and* quantity, and in the ever-resulting inflation generated by the above two situations.

Thus, as the age-old question goes, "So what are we to do?"

We can do several things . . . as parents, as overseers of the younger generation, and as workers ourselves:

Realize the seriousness of today's situation.

Understand that wide spread workforce turnover hurts everyone involved . . . from the CEO, through management, through front line workers, and finally to the consumer.

Consider that a lot of people want a job, but many of them do not want to work.

Teach our young people that business is begging for workers with a good work ethic and a willingness to learn.

Recognize that manufacturing work need not have a negative image among the overall population.

Appreciate that companies cannot continue to pay higher wages, yet remain in the competitive market.

It is our society we are discussing. It is our economic future we are focusing upon. It is the world in which we must live. And we must be able to live *with* it and *in* it.

Overcoming Barriers to Change

If we can count on one element of our society to remain constant, it is the element of change. Some of us face change as a challenge and gingerly look forward to it with enthusiasm and a sense of adventure. We are ready to see what is on the other side of the mountain.

Others of us face change with a sense of fear and trepidation that is paramount to meeting an alien or a feared enemy. And it is certainly true that the older we become, the less we want the world around us to change. We don't care what is on the other side of the mountain. We are on *this* side of the mountain, and that is all we care about.

We must remind ourselves that people *are* capable of changing their behavior, and that if they are made part of that changing process, it will go more smoothly. One person cannot force another person to change. The desire or willingness to change must come from within, but that internal motivation can often come from the realization that if we do not change **with** the times, they will change **without** us. And we will be left behind, standing in the dust of our own stubbornness. This can affect our personal progress, our interpersonal relationships, and even our very livelihood in the employment world.

The Chinese word for CHANGE is comprised of two characters that mean "danger" and "opportunity." If we take the first letter of each of those two words, we have the interesting action verb DO. We must do our part in accepting the reality of change. It is true, nonetheless, that there is a sense of danger in change. It involves the unknown . . . something that is unfamiliar to us. And that creates a sense of apprehension in many people. But change also involves opportunity . . . an occasion to try something new, to learn something different, and the freedom to expand our horizons of thought and activity.

As we face change in our lives, we must take time to evaluate the situation in its entirety. We must first ask ourselves whether or not we are intimidated by the danger involved. If so, we must honestly face that intimidation if we are to move beyond it.

Second, we must realize that if we allow the intimidation to stop us, we will miss the opportunities that also await us.

And last, we must ask ourselves if we are willing to endure the change process although it may mean the discomfort, distress, and confusion of an identity crisis. Most experts say that it takes six weeks to institute a change in our life patterns.

We often forget the presence of an identity crisis as we pass from being the person we are *now* to the person we will *become* at the end of the process. We might say that, during the process, we will become our "new selves."

But as we contemplate this *new self,* we must be willing to accept the persistence that will be required during the identity crisis phase. We must also realize that we must practice the new attitudes and behaviors of accepting a new role. During this time, we can take comfort in the fact that, at the end of our changing process, we will be making fewer mistakes, our fear of change will disappear, and we will become the desired person with the new skill.

We know from past experience that, as our new identity emerges, we will feel progressively more comfortable with that role. We also know from past experience that, as we feel more comfortable with the *new* role, the *old* role will feel more **un**comfortable. We can also take comfort in the fact that we will have increased our self respect, for we accepted a challenge and have seen it through to its completion. We can feel pride in that accomplishment.

But lest we think our entire being will enjoy the "change" ride, we must remember that our subconscious mind will throw obstacles in our path as a means of attempting to make us turn away from the uncertain path ahead. We may suddenly find ourselves believing that the required tasks are too difficult, the technology involved requires more of us than we are capable of producing, our age will make the learning task more difficult, and/or other individuals are making the change more effectively or more quickly than we are. All of these are mind traps generated by self-doubt. We must be prepared for them.

In the late 1960s, Elizabeth Kubler-Ross explained the sequence of steps that individuals experience as they suffer the various traumas in life. And today, those same five steps are being applied to the rapidly changing world in which we live, both in our personal lives and in the workplace.

The first phase is **denial**. As we initially face a required change, we tell ourselves that it is not absolutely necessary to face that change . . . that somehow we will avoid it.

Second, we experience the **anger** of seeing that, indeed, the change *is* required. Following the anger, we experience the **bargaining** stage whereby we attempt to find alternative strategies around what we feel will be inevitable.

Then we find that **depression** often sets in as we experience the "helpless victim" syndrome of being forced into an undesired situation. But finally we experience the **acceptance** of the situation as it truly is. And it is in this final stage that we begin moving forward in a positive and productive manner.

There is much wisdom in the old adage, "To be forewarned is to be forearmed." Having been forewarned of the reactions, responses, and realities of change, we are now ready to not only begin our journey into change . . . to deal with, and accept, the risk involved . . . but also to anticipate and enjoy the opportunities that await us.

We are now ready to see the other side of the mountain.

Is It Right to Be Left?

Cross-cultural studies show approximately 90% of all individuals use their right hand exclusively. Studying right-left preference among animals, dogs, cats, mice, and monkeys has been the subject of extensive studies. Although animals show a paw preference, they are evenly split in their left-or-right preference.

Historical perspectives of left-handedness cast a shadow on the very nature of our "south paw" friends by often referring to them as *sinistrels*. The term *"south paw"* has some unconscious implications. The southern residents of our nation are more slowly paced in their daily lives, and the term *paw* is used when referring to animals rather than humans. And even our modern-day vocabulary paints the left-handed person as somehow deficient. The Italian word for left-handed is "mancino" which also means *deceitful*. In French, the word is "gauche," meaning *clumsy*. And the Spanish word "zurdo," if found in the idiom "no ser zurdo," means *to be very clever*. But the literal translation is *"not to be left-handed."*

Roget's Thesaurus lists several synonyms for "left-handedness" such as *unskillfulness, awkward, backhanded, heavy-handed,* and *clumsy*.

Many theories have abounded over the years as to the significance of being right- or left-handed. One such theory is that the right-of-the-vertical-mid-line placement of several internal organs of the human body places our center of gravity slightly to the right. This would explain why research shows that most humans are able to balance better on their left foot.

Thomas Carlyle, the English essayist and historical writer, recorded that most soldiers held their shields in their left hands to more effectively protect their hearts. Such action would then leave the right hand free, and, over an extended period of time, the muscles in the right arm and hand would become better developed for the finer motor skills necessary in daily living.

The topic of genetics has long been discussed as a determining factor in handedness, thus prompting research into this area. Findings from the *Journal of Heredity* reveal that the probability of two right-handed parents having a left-handed child is two percent. However, that figure rises to 19 percent if one parent is left-handed, and to 46 percent if both parents are left-handed. It appears evident that heredity certainly plays a role in determining handedness, but we must also consider the significant influence of environmental factors as well. These figures account for 54 percent of right-handed children being born to two right-handed parents, according to this study.

Perhaps the placement of paper draws our attention to many left-handed writers. Due to the customary right-handed placement of paper slanting toward the left that was used during earlier days of traditional American education, the inverted hand position was the only way in which such writers could see what they were writing. Fortunately, in today's educational circles, paper placement and hand preference are considered when teaching young children the fundamentals of writing.

Some of the more famous left-handed people include:

Leonardo da Vinci, Italian artist and inventor
Kim Novak, U.S. actress
Babe Ruth, U.S. baseball player
Rex Harrison, British actor
George II, king of England
Michelangelo, Italian artist
Cole Porter, U.S. composer
Charlie Chaplin, British actor and director
Danny Kaye, U.S. actor and comedian
Harry S. Truman, U.S. President

Jimmy Connors, U.S. tennis player
Harpo Marx, U.S. comedian
Marie Dionne, one of the Canadian quintuplets
James Corbett, U.S. heavyweight boxing champion
Carl Philipp Emanuel Bach, German composer
Terence Stamp, British actor
Judy Garland, U.S. actress and singer
Sandy Koufax, U.S. baseball pitcher

Two famous men, Horatio Nelson (British naval officer) and Thomas Carlyle (British essayist and historian) became left-handed after losing their right hands. This illustrates the tremendous ability of the brain and body to re-learn when circumstances deem it necessary.

Thus, after we study the scientific and social ramifications of hand preference, we realize there are many elements involved in such preference . . . some of which can be tested and measured . . . some of which cannot. But we are still faced with the question, "Is it right to be left?"

Or does it really matter if we are *right* or *left*? For if we accomplish the same task equally well in a different manner, should it be of any real consequence?

Lindberg's Glory

****

Lindberg's Glory

****

New York Daily Mirror

June 15, 1927

These were the headlines of the *Daily Mirror*, New York's best picture newspaper on the occasion of Lindberg's successful solo flight across the Atlantic Ocean. Reporters announced that Lindberg was the quiet kid who hopped the Atlantic as nonchalantly as most of the world's citizens would cross the street to buy a pound of butter. Seventy years have passed since that eventful day, and we wonder within ourselves what "Lucky Lindy" would say about today's air travel, both by plane and spaceship.

According to official police estimates, an approximated 4,300,000 persons shouting and cheering from curbs, windows, and rooftops welcomed their Son of America home to terra firma after his adventure as **America's Air Ambassador.** (Less than 1,000 persons had bade him farewell as he began his journey.)

It is reported that Lindberg "blackened Broadway with humanity and whitened it with ticker tape" as the small bits of paper floated upward as high as 3,000 feet into the air. The aviators who escorted the guest of honor reported that it was like flying through a snowstorm. But no one appeared to truly object to such flying conditions.

Colonel Charles A. Lindberg had begun his quest to conquer the Atlantic with the quiet observation, "I'm going to try to do it just as if it were my regular mail run." Upon his return, Lindberg could not understand the pomp and circumstance that surrounded him, feeling only that he had done his job, hopefully well.

The public, along with reporting media personnel, were surprised to see Lindy appearing before them not in the customary uniform with the colonel's insignia and medals he had received from four nations, but rather "in a blue suit . . . as just one of the people, this boy before whom kings and queens had fawned." Obviously, this man of the sky had returned demonstrating the same humble spirit with which he left.

We are told that 8,000 of New York's "finest" police officers maintained remarkable order, and that amidst the throngs of humanity and the difficulties that are generated from such crowds, only one fatality was reported. An eighteen-year-old young woman named Millie Smitty dropped dead from excitement.

A number of the spectators were creative in their solution of dealing with the terrible heat generated by such a mass of humanity pushed together. Many creative souls simply climbed into trees and enjoyed the spectacle from their enviable perch. One ardent admirer went so far as to climb a lamp post along the main route of the parade so he could get what he called a "Wow!" of a view.

Lindberg's mother, who was on hand for the festivities, declared that her son's future was in his own hands. "I have no plans for him," she said.

The American flag was held in high esteem on that glorious day as the daily picture editorial displayed "Old Glory" blowing in the breeze, emblazoned with the following words on the white stripes:

> Freedom
> Prosperity
> Equality
> Peace
> Tolerance
> Opportunity

Quoted from the *Daily Mirror*, an accompanying salute praised "Old Glory's Day" by reminding readers that:

"TODAY WE HONOR THE FLAG
of our country

BECAUSE it flew in far places in those early days when the sturdy pioneers were carving out of the wilderness our nation of today —

BECAUSE it waves from the flagstaffs along the stupendous skylines of the world's most marvelous cities; and over thousands of school-houses where are growing up the land's coming citizens —

BECAUSE it has shrouded the illustrious dead fallen in many wars fought for the perpetuation of American ideals, and floats over their lasting resting places at home and abroad."

In his column titled "Uncommon Sense," Jack Blake made the following observation concerning emulation:

"To equal or surpass what has been done by man is a natural instinct, and it arises not from jealousy or a desire for distinction, but from a realization of one's own ability that might never have been awakened had not some achievement revealed its possibility.

"Emulation has lifted men out of themselves, taught them what they could do, and instilled them with the industry to do it.

"One of the noblest of human attributes is that of emulation.

"Without it we should be a sordid, money grabbing crowd, with no other motives but to feather our own nests."

As we read of such noble and lofty motivation, we must ask ourselves, "Would Mr. Blake re-think his position if he were to visit our society today?"

Further on in the newspaper, readers were informed that a 67-year-old Jamaican man was sentenced to Sing Sing for life. His crime? Stealing six chickens and six ducks.

Of course, no paper, regardless of national events, would be complete without its advertisements. A few of them include:

GIMBELS - GREATER DOWNSTAIRS

Placed on Sale for the First Time —

8150 VOILE DRESSES

Fresh, new summery styles — sale priced

10 Styles from Which to Select

$1.88

Limited Quantities of Sizes 36 to 46

****

Feel Dizzy?

Headachy, billious, constipated?

Take **NR** - NATURE'S REMEDY - tonight.
This mild, safe, vegetable remedy will have you
feeling fine by morning.

At Druggists — only 25 cents

****

Give *me* Chiclets . . . *every time*
ALWAYS *Pure & Fresh*

The quality candy-coated gum in the handy box

5 cents

****

219

A Walk through the Cemetery: Part I

We all have a place on the map that we call HOME. In my case, it's a little town on the bend of the Ohio River where Ohio, Pennsylvania, and West Virginia meet in what is typically referred to as the Tri-State Area of eastern Ohio.

East Liverpool is not a large town, although it was considered to be one of the pottery centers of the world at the turn of the century. Specially preserved kilns may be seen at various spots throughout the city . . . a quiet testimony to the pottery heritage of the past.

This little burg sits at the foothills of the Pennsylvania and West Virginia hills, and the contour of the land is an interesting study in steep, mile-long hills that provide interesting travel during the winter months of snow-and-ice-covered roads.

Sitting atop one of the hills in East Liverpool is Riverview Cemetery, appropriately named for its scenic view of the river below. Riverview is immaculately manicured, and a drive through its winding roads can be a pleasant and relaxing escape from the hectic pace of the outside world. In fact, many local people use the picturesque cemetery roads to accommodate their walking and exercise programs.

I walked through the cemetery recently and took time to appreciate its quiet beauty. As I walked, I took special note of a number of the tombstones and the lives they represented.

I saw a headstone with an oval colored portrait of a young sailor attached to the granite. The birth and death dates indicate he died in the prime of life. I wonder what happened. I wonder if his parents ever recovered from the pain of losing a son who was probably full of life.

I saw five small flat markers with the names of a mother and father, along with three young children. The death years are not the same, and I can only imagine the circumstances surrounding such losses.

I saw large, towering monuments inscribed with names of leading prominent citizens of the community. Some of these family plots seemed as if they were miniature parks unto themselves. One such area contained a granite bench. I wonder if anyone ever sits on that bench? Or is its purpose purely ornamental?

I saw the marker of a familiar grave . . . a twelve-year-old neighbor boy I knew had died after seven months of lingering in a coma when a virus attacked his brain.

I saw the marker of a young mother who had been the victim of cancer. And the marker of another young woman who had been the victim of a blood clot after surgery.

I saw a marker with a lamb sculptured across the top. A baby had been laid to rest there.

I saw American names. I saw foreign names.

I saw names of old folks. I saw names of young children.

I saw names of soldiers.

Each name . . . each marker . . . represented a life, a loss.

But one tombstone in particular has always been of interest to me. One side of a large marker is gray granite. The other side is black. An interesting account surrounds this marker that I have heard since I was a child. As the story goes, a couple had married and discovered that they simply could not live together in the same house. Neither did they want to completely part ways. As a result, they moved into a "double house." This was the terminology of yesteryear for a house that consisted of two distinct halves, each with their own living accommodations . . . and having a dividing wall in the substructure of the dwelling.

The story continues that the man and woman each lived in

their respective half of the house until their deaths. They had been *together*, yet *separate*. And they continued in death as in life, each having his and her respective half of the tombstone. But the division in their lives was marked in death by the division in the differently colored granite.

I have been tempted on several occasions to seek out the truth of this particular story. But something always prohibits me from investigating.

Perhaps it is the intrigue of such an account.

Perhaps it is the mystery that surrounds the possibility of two people living under such circumstances.

Perhaps it is the reminder that it takes conscious effort on the part of all persons involved in a relationship to keep that relationship alive and well . . . that it must be nurtured and fed as plants and animals.

Perhaps it is the reminder that, unless careful consideration is given to a relationship, the people involved will simply go their separate ways and live in two different worlds . . . in two different "houses" as it were. And if the separation continues to grow deeply enough and wide enough, the poor victims involved could qualify for *together, yet separate,* tombstones.

Sad, but in this case, ***true.***

A Walk through the Cemetery: Part II

I ended my thoughtful journey with stopping by my family plot of graves. And from that large marker, I took time to recapture special memories from the past of the loved ones lying there.

I saw my mother's name. She was a woman of many talents . . . registered nurse, published author, public speaker, radio program moderator, and a friend to those who truly needed a friend at the difficult times in their lives. But in the midst of her time-consuming responsibilities, Mama never forgot her two top priorities . . . her Christian walk and her family. She served her church, her community, and her loved ones in countless ways. But she never waited around to receive thanks. Feeling good about what she did was all the thanks she ever expected.

As a little girl, I spent the Christmas holidays delivering home-made banana bread and cookies with my mother to those individuals she wanted to surprise with freshly baked goodies. But the neatest part about Mama was that she continued to do acts of kindness for those around her during the entire year.

She passed away when I was only 33 years old and expecting my third child. I missed her deeply during those long, last months of my pregnancy. I missed her deeply when Mark was finally born. And I miss her deeply now after 20 years. She was not only my mother, but my very best friend. I could have used her wise counsel many times during the years I have been raising my own children. Although she has been absent in the body for the past two decades, she has been present in spirit . . . and continues to be so even during the writing of this book. She always believed I had inherited some of her writing skills, and she often told me that she thought I had a book in me somewhere.

Then I saw my father's name. He was a man of many moods and was extremely difficult to live with. None of us ever knew when the stormy part of him would break forth as a raging tornado and disrupt everyone's life. But, in spite of his shortcomings, he had a tender heart for people in need, and he would often extend his automotive repair services to those who could not pay. Or if the charges were simply too much for him to absorb, he would charge the customer only wholesale parts/materials prices, while donating a portion or all of his labor.

I think Daddy was perhaps a victim of his own background, much as he made those around him victims. As I learned more about Daddy's background, I realized the explosive venom his own father spit out upon those around him. I remember how Grandpa would lash out in such anger to the people who cared most about him. I remember how Grandpa would *demand* his own way, regardless of the cost to family and friends. Also, suddenly I realized that Daddy, who was the oldest child, probably caught the brunt of most of his father's anger. Finally I came to understand that my father was truly a product of his environment and that he had been either *unwilling* or *unable* to break the devastating chains of behavior he had learned as a child.

I moved on to Grandma's name. That dear old German lady who was my mother's mother had made her two grandchildren feel they were the most important people in the world. She helped shape our moral convictions and reminded us that we had a responsibility to ourselves, our family, and our community to be the very best people we could be. She loved us unconditionally, but she also made us tow the line when we were with her. There was nothing fancy or frilly about Grandma . . . just wonderful, open concern for those nearby. I had the privilege of visiting with Grandma just three weeks before her death. She was in excellent health for a woman 90 years old, and we reminisced over old times for the entire weekend. Over the years, she had continued to do all her own house cleaning and her own canning. Five days after our visit ended, she suffered a stroke and lay in a coma for three weeks before passing away.

Although I could not be with her during those three weeks, I had the folks at the hospital put the phone to her ear, and I took the opportunity to tell her a few last times how much I had appreciated and loved her down through the years. I will never know if Grandma ever heard me during those phone calls, and the hospital personnel did not know. But I was able to take comfort in the fact that I had also told Grandma how I felt many times *before* she suffered the stroke. They were my roses to her while she lived.

And then there was Grandpap's name. He was a neat guy. He and Grandma made a good pair. Perhaps the funniest conversation I ever had with Grandpap was the day he was 95 years old and complained about having arthritis in his knees. I suppose I was shocked by his complaint, for he was otherwise in good physical condition. I told him that when I became his age, I probably wouldn't *have* any knees. And then I reminded him he was 95 years old. He looked at me, laughed, and said, "So what? What does my age have to do with it?" And he was serious. Age was totally irrelevant to Grandpap. Perhaps that is why he had continued to rabbit hunt into his seventies and to grow his tomato plants and rose garden into his mid-eighties.

The men with whom Grandpap hunted finally had to stop going with him. All the other men would stop and rest part way through the hunt. They would also let the dogs rest. But **no one** could make Grandpap stop and rest. And the other men, fearful they would find Grandpap lying in a ravine somewhere from a heart attack, began making excuses not to hunt with him any longer. My dad's beagles could even distinguish Grandpap's walk, and they would begin barking as he came up the alley behind our home. It was not the typical dog bark alerting those nearby of someone approaching. It was the excited beagle howl that said, "He's here. It's time to go chase the rabbits!" They did this for no one but Grandpap. He and they seemed to have a special bond of affection for one another.

Grandpap and I agreed on his 95th birthday that, regardless of where I was in the country, I would return home for his 100th birthday party. But that party was not meant to be. He passed away at age 97, completely in charge of his mental faculties and living with his other daughter (my aunt) until five days before his death when a stroke also took him from us.

And then I came to my aunt's name. She was my mother's sister, but they looked nothing alike. Yet in temperament and life's priorities, they were like two peas in a pod. They were best of friends, and they spent many good years together. I remember Aunt Dee and my mother having "discussions" on many occasions. But they were not the normal discussions between two sisters who disagree. These conversations always focused on each sister trying to give the best of whatever was under consideration to the other sister. The "look out for number one" in this relationship meant looking out for each other. And both my aunt and my mother extended this same loving consideration to my grandmother. They made a great trio, and I learned a lot of life's lessons at the feet of those three ladies!

But perhaps the greatest pain came from the name on the tombstone of our first-born infant daughter. She was just ready to begin her life when it was taken from her. Her unexpected death threw our world into violent reverse. Then, in the weeks and months ahead, we learned to cope with our world coming to a deathly quiet stop. We were shocked that everyone's life continued on and that the sun continued to shine. Our world had been shattered, but the universe continued to function as always. Nothing different. Yet nothing the same.

There are three names on the family marker whose graves are not yet occupied . . . my uncle's, my husband's, and my own. Uncle Kenny is still with us, and we enjoy his company at every opportune moment, although 400 miles separate us. He is the kind of man every young person would want for a role model, and we appreciate our times together.

Several people have asked me if I am bothered by seeing my name on a tombstone. I assure them I am not. I know within my heart that dying is part of living. That death follows birth. Sometimes it follows quickly. Sometimes it does not come for decades.

But it does come.

Of that we can be certain.

But as I stood at my family's monument in Riverview Cemetery in that little town on the bend of the Ohio River, I did not focus upon my name being written on cold, hard granite. Rather I placed my attention upon my life and influence being written in my everyday existence. Each day, I am given the privilege of enjoying the beauty and the bounty around me. I am given the opportunity to again make a difference in the world around me. I am blessed with another occasion to lend a helping hand to the harried and the hurting people who are in such large supply in our world today.

And I am given suitable occasions for exercising my freedom of choice.

Freedom to choose whether my past memories will be laden with anger and hurt . . . or whether they will be laden with love and appreciation.

Freedom to choose whether my present will focus upon my own needs and desires . . . or whether it will focus upon the needs and desires of those around me .

Freedom to choose whether my future will be absorbed by

thoughts of how the world made a better place in which **I** could live . . . or whether I made the world a better place in which **others** could live!

I am free to make choices . . .

I am NOT free

    to escape

        the *consequences*

            of those choices!

                And neither are any of us!

To My "Family" at Boyce Church

It is because of the faithful witness of many of you at Boyce Church that I am where I am today in my spiritual walk. I remember growing up under the consistent, daily Christian witness of precious people like Clyde and Hilda, Howard and Ruth, Joe and Margaret, Chillie and Lois, Chuck and Norma, Ralph and Thelma, and Delmar and Mable. I remember growing up under the faithful influence of so many other special people who continue to have an influence in my life. We were not bound by blood and genetics, but by something much stronger . . . a relationship we will treasure throughout all of eternity.

I shall be forever reminded of Dottie's strength and courage as she unfailingly took her place of ministry at the organ while raising three boys. I shall always remember Katie's radiant smile from the choir loft. I shall never forget Bonnie's willingness to keep the Sunday School records year after year, never complaining of the paperwork involved.

It was not what these people SAID that caught my attention; it was what they DID in their faithful service to their church and to their Lord. I watched them as their faith stayed strong during the difficult times. I loved them because they always seemed to have time for the kid at 1642 Pennsylvania Avenue who climbed too many trees, always had skinned knees, and talked too much in church . . . and in school . . . and most everywhere else, actually.

I do not think we will ever know in this life how much influence Boyce Church has had on the world. Only as each of us stand before God will we realize the impact of the small community church . . . this small church that had such a large impact as we attempted to share our love and faith with those we encountered along life's path.

I watched over the years as our older members suffered through years of prolonged illness. I watched while babies and young mothers were called home to Heaven. And I found myself trying to make sense of it all. My pondering brought me to only one conclusion . . . at those times in life when things seem unjust, unfair, and unequal, we must trust in God's goodness and sovereignty. And we must remember that He never makes a mistake.

When I complained of having to sit in an uncomfortable church pew for three hours on Good Friday one year, my mother was the one who pulled me up short with, "If you are uncomfortable sitting in a pew, think how uncomfortable Christ was hanging on the cross." It wasn't said in anger or mocking, but I never complained about sitting in church again.

So many years have gone by, so many events have taken place. So many loved ones are waiting for the greatest reunion known to mankind at the portals of Heaven. So many miles separate us. Yet in spite of it all, I so vividly recall my growing-up years being punctuated by words and acts of kindness from so many special people who remain alive in my spirit long after their deaths.

I grew up in Boyce Church. It is where I learned the Christian principles by which I still live my life. It is where I was married in 1967. It is where I heart-brokenly entered for worship a few weeks after the death of our first child in 1972. It is where I had my second daughter dedicated in 1974. It is where I later brought my son and attempted to recall some of my memories for him. It is where I still visit on our trips to East Liverpool . . . that little pottery town on the bend of the Ohio River that I shall forever call HOME.

And to each of you, I leave the following encouraging words:

When you cannot rejoice in your emotions,

When you cannot rejoice in your situation,

*Rejoice in the fact that God is **still** God . . .*

*that He is **still** on the throne . . .*

*and that He is **still** in control!*

Dear Reader:

And Another Thing . . . about Living, Loving, and Learning is, of course, the companion to *I've Been Thinking . . . about Living, Loving, and Learning.* If you have had the opportunity to read both volumes, I trust that you found each of them thought-provoking and helpful in their own unique way.

Andrew Wyeth, perhaps the greatest American painter of this century, once observed, "I can't work completely out of my imagination. I must put my foot in a bit of truth, and then I can fly free." I could not have expressed that sentiment more appropriately, for I, too, must experience the reality of life before my literary imagination can be sparked by creativity.

What has *And Another Thing . . . about Living, Loving, and Learning* sparked in your own mind, spirit, soul, or heart? If you have experienced something special in reading these pages, would you please write and tell me about it? Please include your full name, address, and complete phone number. Some of these responses may be shared in my other writings, and I want to be able to contact you for permission to use your reply.

Send all correspondence to:

> Alpha Publishing
> A division of Alpha Consulting
> c/o Carol G. Heizer
> P.O. Box 18433
> Louisville, KY 40261-0433

Thanks! And have a good life . . . day by day!

Order Form:

Please send check or money order to:

Carol Heizer
P.O. Box 18433
Louisville, KY 40261-0433

ITEM	PRICE	TOTAL PRICE
And Another Thing ... about Living, Loving, and Learning	____ @ $12.95 Each *BOOK*	
I've Been Thinking ... about Living, Loving, and Learning	____ @ $12.95 Each *BOOK*	
I've Been Thinking ... about Living, Loving, and Learning	____ @ $9.95 Each *TAPE*	
It's a Matter of Life and Death	____ @ $12.95 Each *BOOK*	
Alternative Education	____ @ $12.95 Each *BOOK*	
Shipping and Handling	1st item $3.00 Each additional item $1.00 Max. $7.00 for 1-10 items	
Sales Tax for Kentucky Residents Orders Outside U.S. Add	6% 25%	
	Grand Total:	

Name _____

Address _____

City _____ State _____

Zip _____ - _____

Phone (_____) _____ - _____

Visit

   Carol

      on the

         World Wide Web

at:

http://www.welcometoalpha.com

Email:
   cgheizer@welcometoalpha.com